VALUES AND EVALUATIONS

VALUES

AND

EVALUATIONS

Z. NAJDER

CLARENDON PRESS · OXFORD
1975

Oxford University Press, Ely House, London W1

GLASGOW NEW YORK TORONTO MELBOURNE WELLINGTON
CAPE TOWN IBADAN NAIROBI DAR ES SALAAM LUSAKA ADDIS ABABA
DELHI BOMBAY CALCUTTA MADRAS KARACHI LAHORE DACCA
KUALA LUMPUR SINGAPORE HONG KONG TOKYO

ISBN 0 19 875035 8

*Printed in Great Britain by
William Clowes & Sons, Limited
London, Beccles and Colchester*

ACKNOWLEDGEMENTS

THIS book owes much to the conversations and correspondence which I have had, at different times within the last fifteen years, with Professors Abraham Kaplan, Sidney Morgenbesser, Charles L. Stevenson, Mieczysław Wallis, and Richard Wollheim. In the sixties, while studying in Oxford and working on the problem of aesthetic evaluation, I profited greatly from my regular meetings with Professor Sir Alfred Ayer. The original Polish version of this book was based on my doctoral dissertation, written under the friendly supervision of Professor Władysław Tatarkiewicz, who helped me to clarify many of my ideas. Professor Jerzy Pelc, who read the manuscript and published two extensive fragments in *Studia Semiotyczne*, was remarkably generous in his valuable comments and advice.

The English version would look much worse if not for the assistance of my friend Professor William Bossart, who endeavoured to make the text more readable and offered innumerable suggestions concerning the way my case is presented. Parts of the English manuscript have been read and corrected also by Mr. Christopher Howells and Mr. Angus Walker. Of course, for whatever errors of thought or language I may have committed, none of these persons, to whom I am deeply grateful, is to be held responsible.

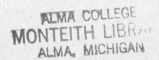

CONTENTS

INTRODUCTION

BOTH the origins and the aims of this theoretical book have been primarily practical. When I began to study philosophy, a few years after the Second World War and a few years before the death of Stalin, choice and justification seemed, even to a youthful enthusiast of logical positivism, the most urgent philosophical issues. In later years I spent much of my time on literary criticism and research, and the omnipresence of problems of evaluation in the methodology of the humanities again and again impressed itself on my mind.

Whatever the merits of contemporary theories of value and evaluation may be, it is easy to see that by and large they are difficult to apply practically outside the realm of philosophy. Instead of facilitating they tend rather to hamper comparative discussion of divergent views, and only seldom make use of methods tested and experiential data gathered by a few interrelated disciplines.

Thus a task presents itself: to work out a conceptual system which could be useful in analysing the logic of evaluative judgements, their testability, their possible cognitive content, and their relations to other kinds of utterances. Such a system would facilitate the use of the results of contemporary social historical and biological sciences and it would also make it easier for specialists in various disciplines to communicate their evaluative problems and pool their experience. To propose and outline such a system is the aim of this book.

It seems clear to me that at least for the present purpose the broadest conceptual framework of logico-empirically oriented philosophy is preferable to other frameworks which do not entertain a close rapport with contemporary social sciences and even with modern historiography.

Although, for reasons which will be shown later, I do not believe that a thorough purge of description and analysis of normative undertones is possible, I have tried to be impartial towards all different theories of value. However, in the context of the modern vogue of utilitarianism, a slight insistence on the 'legitimacy' of non-utilitarian and, more broadly, non-pragmatic kinds of value may be discerned here. The reason for this insistence is not that I believe that values like fidelity are 'higher', but because I think adherence to them is too often overlooked, and also because I grew up in a time and a place where values of the non-pragmatic sort showed themselves to be outstandingly important.

Some fragments of this book were written, and a few published, as early as 1961–2. The whole text was completed in late 1969 and published in Poland in 1971. The English version is not exactly a translation but rather an expanded adaptation. I have replaced certain examples with ones more familiar or accessible to the English reader. Several points have been clarified and amplified, and a few new sections added. Also, I have tried to bring the text up to date by discussing issues raised by some more recent publications.

Translation of a contemporary philosophical piece offers some insight into the question as to what extent philosophical problems belong to a given language. I firmly believe that all the more important ones transcend language barriers. Even if they are language-bound, they are not bound to any one language. Still, transporting ideas from one language into another is a tricky business. There is little worry if the vocabulary of the language into which one translates is, in the given field, richer than the vocabulary of the original: this is the case with English verbs which are markedly more numerous than Polish verbs. The situation is worse if the opposite prevails—such as is the case with abstract nouns and adjectives, which are in much shorter supply in English than in Polish.

I cannot list here all the difficulties encountered, but two terminological decisions have to be explained. 'Valuation' and 'to value' are ambiguous terms, as they may signify both acts and attitudes. I shall restrict the use of these words to contexts which refer to attitudes and states; in talking about acts, judgements, and procedures, on the other hand, I use the words 'evaluation' and 'evaluate'. In contrast to other European languages, English tends to limit the meaning of 'science' to what are called elsewhere the 'exact sciences'. This historically and intellectually interesting custom causes a lot of trouble, as there is no common name for other kinds of systematized knowledge, and as it is becoming more and more difficult to decide what is exact science and what is not; many disciplines, for instance psychology, have to be partitioned. For the purposes of this book the unity of science (to invoke that old watchword of the New Positivism) is much more important than its internal divisions. Therefore I have decided to use 'science', and 'scientific', as comprehensive terms, referring to mathematical, natural and social sciences as well as to the humanities—in other words, as counterparts of 'nauka', 'Wissenschaft', 'scienza', and so on.

As the aims of this book are integrative and its scope inter-disciplinary, it is addressed not only to those interested in the philosophy of value; but also to students of ethics, aesthetics, sociology, law, history, methodology of the humanities, and related disciplines.

Most of the examples discussed come from the field of ethics, but aesthetic problems occupy quite a large place. This is because the status of aesthetic judgements has given rise to an unusually large number of doubts and debates. Therefore it seemed that, if one were able to demonstrate that a reasoned discussion on the validity of aesthetic evaluations is possible, such a possibility could, *a fortiori*, be considered as applying to other kinds of value-judgements.

CHAPTER I

EVALUATION

§1. *Evaluation and knowledge*

Knowing is inseparable from evaluation. This is true of both 'external' and 'internal' reality, of perceptions and sensations as well as of intellectual and scientific understanding. It is commonly acknowledged that our consciousness acts selectively upon the great mass of stimuli absorbed by our sensory organs. This selection is carried out at many levels: through psychophysiological dispositions, conditioned reflexes, anticipations, habits—and also, at the level of opinions, regarding what is and what is not worth noticing, what is important and valuable and what insignificant and valueless.[1] The data, assimilated by our consciousness, are sorted out by the mind; in this process again evaluation is an important factor. Objects can be classed according to their size or colour, familiarity or strangeness; frequently we class them according to our conception of their value.

The so-called 'empirical' or 'descriptive' criteria for arrangement and classification most frequently emerge to be closely linked with the evaluative ones. A combination of both kinds of criteria forms the basis of deciding whether a given object is a house or a shanty; a given animal a horse or a jade; a given activity, work or bustle; whether a certain gentleman is bald or not, etc. Indeed, borderline cases are typically decided by application of assessment: to solve the problem of how a given object is to be classified, the set of defining characteristics is enriched by adding evaluative determinants. Thus we decide whether a decrepit metal contraption on wheels is still a car or is a wreck. Another example may be

[1] From among plentiful psychological and physiological evidence it is worth referring specifically to J. Konorski's theory of 'gnostic units' and 'fields'. Formation and organization of gnostic fields, the basic factors in perception, are closely related to the interests of the given subject. See Jerzy Konorski, *Integrative Activity of the Brain* (Chicago, 1967), pp. 73–6.

deciding to which literary genre a given piece belongs: a bad classical tragedy is, presumably, always a tragedy; but will we apply this name to a poor drama, written according to the Romantic recipes of 'fragmentary' poetics?

We have now passed to problems connected with science and scholarship. Gunnar Myrdal wrote:

This implicit belief in the existence of a body of scientific knowledge acquired independently of all valuations is, as I now see it, naïve empiricism. Facts do not organize themselves into concepts and theories just by being looked at; indeed, except within the framework of concepts and theories, there are no scientific facts but only chaos. There is an inescapable *a priori* element in all scientific work. Questions must be asked before answers can be given. The questions are an expression of our interest in the world, they are at bottom valuations. Valuations are thus necessarily involved already at the stage when we observe facts and carry on theoretical analysis, and not only at the stage when we draw political inferences from facts and valuations.[1]

The role of evaluative factors in scientific understanding has been in this century a frequent object of scrutiny, undertaken from various methodological positions. Thus for instance Charles L. Stevenson, a philosopher belonging to the positivist tradition and therefore in principle inclined to differentiate sharply between, if not to oppose, description and evaluation, admits that 'No inquiry . . . can divorce itself from the evaluative considerations that directly concern and guide the process of inquiry itself'.[2] However, he limits the role of the evaluative element to that of 'organizing knowledge'[3] and takes no account of difficulties that arise when one tries to distinguish which fundamental assumptions of our scientific interests and methods are, and which are not, based on valuation.

A few examples will illustrate the point. Edwin A. Burtt in *The Metaphysical Foundations of Modern Physical Science* lays bare the 'metaphysical' premises tacitly or sometimes openly assumed by

---

[1] G. Myrdal, Preface to *The Political Element in the Development of Economic Theory* (London, 1953), p. vii.

[2] C. L. Stevenson, *Ethics and Language* (New Haven, Conn., 1944), p. 161.

[3] Ibid., p. 286: 'There are certain evaluative issues that are integral to the very process of organizing knowledge.'

Copernicus, Galileo, Kepler, Newton, and others.[1] Burtt's book was published in 1924, before the philosophers of science began to consider seriously the possibility that in the choice of a scientific method or theory conscious or unconscious valuation might play a role. When we look a little closer at these premisses revealed by Burtt, we are inclined to conclude that they can frequently be described as beliefs about values. Some of the explanations offered by Burtt and concerning, for example, the genesis of a new methodological standpoint adopted by Copernicus, sound similar to Lucien Goldmann's views on the foundations of Durkheim's theories. Goldmann's main thesis is that any scholarly work in the humanities, theoretical as well as concretely descriptive, is consciously or unconsciously grounded in the author's evaluative assumptions.[2] It is not clear, however, whether Goldmann maintains that the link between evaluative foundations and the content of a given work has the character of a socio-psychological necessity (i.e., since the author is a member of a certain class, he simply cannot think differently), or whether the connection is logical (i.e., with particular evaluative assumptions there must be connected definite theories and methods and, inversely, every theory or method requires given evaluative assumptions). Goldmann seems to suggest the first possibility, but his examples would support rather the latter, more cautious version. This version is not unlike Friedrich Meinecke's much earlier statement that in historical research there is an indissoluble link between values and 'the knowledge of causes and effects'.[3]

If the example of Goldmann sounds frivolous to some, an entirely serious one may be adduced in the case of Karl Popper. His ideas about the origins, psychological and methodological, of scientific hypotheses clearly support the view that valuations give an initial push to our scientific interests and thinking.[4] Philipp

[1] E. A. Burtt, *The Metaphysical Foundations of Modern Physical Science* (Chicago, 1924).

[2] L. Goldmann, *The Human Sciences and Philosophy* (London, 1969), pp. 35–50.

[3] F. Meinecke, 'Kausalitäten und Werte in der Geschichte' (1928), in *Staat und Persönlichkeit* (Berlin, 1933), p. 29.

[4] K. Popper, *Conjectures and Refutations* (London, 1963), p. 6.

Frank also has demonstrated the inescapable role of extra-scientific factors—primarily evaluations—in decisions accepting or rejecting the most general theories in science. One of these factors is the 'capacity to foster a desirable way of life'.[1] Finally, Maria Ossowska has made a special study of the necessary place of evaluation in the formation of at least some scientific concepts.[2]

§2. Evaluation as experience : motivational pattern of valuations

2.1 'Evaluation' may mean the same as 'evaluative experience', i.e., it may designate a certain type of psychical process, a kind of apperception. One can talk about both individual and collective apperception—with reference to racial prejudice, for example, or changes of fashion; to avoid the danger of hypostatizing it, it is more convenient to use individual examples.

Looking at the landscape from a moving car one judges it to be pretty, or inhospitable, or spoiled by industry, etc. In remembering friends, recollecting their behaviour, one tends to recall them in value-laden terms. Such remembrances leave behind them a more or less definite mood, they constitute an emotional assessment of the given person. Experiences of horror and resentment, enchantment and admiration, are evaluative experiences. When we imagine ourselves to be prisoners, this psychical act is also a form of valuation. Except in atypical cases, as when we simply search for a quotation, we must class as evaluative our experiences when reading a novel, listening to a concert, looking at a film or a painting. Our attention is then focused on satisfaction or frustration, liking or disliking, being moved or remaining indifferent. When we 'contemplate', it is important whether our contemplation remains undisturbed, whether unexpected elements are justified by the overall construction of the work, etc. A deeper penetration into the object of our perception, closer listening to a piece of music, prolonged scrutiny of a painting, rereading of a poem—all are usually aimed at a more adequate appreciation of the given object or experience. The same applies to meditations on human character or

[1] P. Frank, *Philosophy of Science* (Garden City, N.J., 1957), pp. 354–9.
[2] M. Ossowska, 'Rola ocen w kształtowaniu pojęć', in *Fragmenty filozoficzne, Księga pamiątkowa ku czci T. Kotarbińskiego* (Warsaw, 1967).

behaviour. Quite frequently also, consciously or not, we compare the contents of a given experience or the impression of an object with analogous experiences and impressions.

On what grounds can we distinguish evaluations as experiences, or evaluative experiences, from other kinds of experiences? It seems impossible to draw a distinction based on the nature of the object of an experience or on its intensity. However, it may be possible to discern their function in man's psychical life. Evaluation is always a preferential ranking of the contents of our experience.[1] When we evaluate, we grade our feelings and sensations, or the impulses which evoked them, as pleasant or unpleasant, desired or undesired, approved or rejected.

2.2 One of the results of evaluation, and the most important for man's functioning, is that it supplies motives for actions.

As we very well know, man's behaviour may be variously motivated.[2] The motive of an action as simple as crossing the street may be habit, or an intention to buy something, a fancy to look at a pretty girl, the wish to avoid meeting someone one dislikes, the desire to walk in the sun or to escape noise, and so on. We know, too, that men react differently to the same stimuli, to natural events such as rain or earthquake, for example, and also that they can influence each other by very different means. If, for instance, I want my son to eat an apple, I may simply order him to

[1] See the programme of research as outlined by Charles Morris in 'Axiology as the Science of Preferential Behavior', in *Value: A Cooperative Inquiry*, ed. Ray Lepley (New York, 1949).

[2] I leave aside the question whether it is possible to subsume all these different motives under uniform rules, as for example under the hedonist principle as formulated by Moritz Schlick (*Problems of Ethics*, New York, 1962, p. 40); or under the principles proposed by the 'general theory of action', explaining human behaviour in terms of prizes and punishments (see G. Homans, *Social Behavior*, New York, 1961, and A. Malewski, *O zastosowaniach teorii zachowania*, Warsaw, 1964); or else under the principle of homeostasis, which, according to C. N. Cofer and M. H. Appley, 'is a basis for a psychology of value' (*Motivation: Theory and Research*, New York, 1964, pp. 325–6; the authors support here the theory of C. A. Mace, expounded in his presidential address to the British Psychological Society in 1953).

The term 'motive' I use in the sense as understood by psychologists: 'The motive for an action is the reason that is actually operative', R. S. Peters, *The Concept of Motivation* (London, 1958), p. 38.

eat it and expect obedience; I may set him an example by eating an apple myself; quote a medical journal which extols the beneficial effects of apple-eating; or tell him how tasty and juicy are these apples on the table.

Most of our conscious actions result from choice. Exceptional situations apart, in which no choice is possible, we are always faced with the possibility of at least a few, probably more than a few, different actions. Often the choice is automatic: we know what to do, and even why we do it, but do not muse about it. Occasionally, however, we ponder over the simplest acts, analysing the reasons that made us behave in a particular way, or weighing up what we should do in the future. It is probable that, among the motives of past actions or motives forming the basis of future behaviour, there will also be evaluative experiences, or conclusions drawn from them in the form of evaluative judgements. For instance: 'I ate that apple because it looked nice'; 'I crossed the street because the sun shone so pleasantly'; 'I shall run after the bus because mother will be sorry if I am late'; 'I shall lend John a fiver because he is an honest chap.' Evaluative experiences and judgements will find their place among other possible motives of action such as commands, habits, physiological needs, and emotional drives.

Psychologists and sociologists claim that human motivations can be categorized in terms of regularities in their occurrence. While it is sometimes difficult to discover or predict the motivation of a particular act, if we deal with a greater number of cases the statistical probability of the recurrence of certain analogous motivations tends to be quite high. Specialists in advertising, educators, propagandists and night-club owners know that very well. Valuations belong among the most stable conscious determinants of motivation. This is so, among other reasons, because valuations, although individually carried out, are an element of social life. In an evaluative experience one takes a position in relation to other people, their works and deeds; a position towards a group, society, mankind. Clyde Kluckhohn wrote: 'Values and motivation are linked. . . . Values are only an element in motivation and in determining action; they invariably have implications for motivation . . . values canalize motivation.'[1]

[1] C. Kluckhohn, 'Values and Value-Orientations in the Theory of Action:

Let us assume that conscious decisions concerning all non-reflex actions are possible, 'conscious' being taken in the sense of one's being aware of other alternative options.[1] Detailed descriptions of such hypothetical situations involving fully conscious choice would reveal that, in the last resort, every choice of one and not another possible way of acting is psychologically grounded in evaluation—even if the agent himself is not aware of such dependence.[2] This arises from two structural features of our conceptual apparatus: 1. we use the fundamental concept of a person as the author of his own actions; 2. normative utterances ('A ought to be done') do not normally follow for us from descriptive statements, but are in our consciousness linked rather to evaluative judgements ('since B is good and A leads to B, A ought to be done'). Therefore, the choice, e.g., whether to cross the street or not, may depend—if we assume that the choice is 'fully conscious'—on whether a greater value is represented for us by the pleasure of looking at a pretty female, or by performing the duty of promptly purchasing a bun.

The acceptance of the provisional hypothesis of full consciousness is justified because it is practically impossible to draw a dividing line between conscious and unconscious motives of an action. From a methodological point of view it is more convenient

---

An Exploration in Definition and Classification', in *Toward a General Theory of Action*, ed. T. Parsons and E. A. Shils (Cambridge, Mass., 1951), p. 400.

[1] But not necessarily believing that he himself would at the given moment be able to act differently than he in fact does; one can, for instance, be aware of the weakness of one's will. The problem of the weak will (Aristotle's *akrasia*) I leave aside here, as well as the fundamental problem of the freedom of will; I do not think these issues are essential for my line of thought and for the proposed terminology. Also, I refrain consciously from introducing a distinction between motives and causes of an action: this is a slippery problem from the borderland of philosophy and psychology.

[2] I have in mind the consciousness of one's having options, and not the consciousness of the real causes of a choice; e.g., Jane has to choose between two jars of marmalade: A costing 8p, and B costing 9p. She decides in favour of A, explaining to herself that a lower price was her motive. However, she in fact chooses A because she had seen this brand in a TV advertisement, and the economic motive she uses for self-justification. She conveniently overlooks the fact that the difference in price is offset by the difference in weight (also marked on jars); advertising has a stronger appeal to her than economy.

and useful, in our case, to disregard this line entirely. This would make it possible to bridge the division between the sciences of man and zoology, and to talk about evaluative experiences as grounds for motivation also in animals. Konrad Lorenz, among others, has shown that a sharp distinction, on the psychological plane, between 'instinctive' and 'conscious' behaviour precludes understanding of many types of human activities.

The pattern of motives of action, that is, their correlations, respective importance, and recurrent configurations, is not only 'permeated' by evaluations in the form of specific motives, but may be seen as, in the last resort, based on evaluation. I propose to call this pattern *the motivational pattern of evaluation*.

Within this pattern evaluative judgements do not perform the function of ascribing or defining values, but the function of shaping values: while influencing our decisions they contribute to changing or stabilizing our evaluative attitudes and our beliefs about values.

Psychological and socio-cultural circumstances determine the degree of regularity of evaluative-motivative connections. The more stable and institutionalized are the needs and aims of a given person or group, the more integrated a group, the more regular and predictable is the motivational pattern of evaluation of that person or group.

§3. *Evaluation as reasoning : theoretical pattern of evaluations*

'Evaluation' may also mean a kind of reasoning. Here is a simple example. George believes that to lie is morally bad, and also that it is morally bad to do conscious harm to somebody's health. While visiting his friends he hears John saying to his mother that he enjoyed the play he saw on Saturday. George knows, however, that on Saturday John did not stir from his flat. He has to classify John's statement as a lie, i.e., a morally reprehensible act. Since he regards John as a veracious person and a loving son, he considers the case and recalls that John has a heart affliction and on Saturday felt particularly shaky. He asks John's wife whether her mother-in-law, an elderly and nervous person, knows of her son's illness, and receives a negative answer. He concludes that John lied to his mother because he did not want to arouse in her any harmful anxiety. As John's lie had no negative effects, the conclusion of George's evaluative reasoning will probably be a judgement that John's behaviour was not morally wrong.

George's beliefs formed the theoretical basis of his reasoning. Evaluative reasoning is impossible without certain general evaluative assumptions. Thus understood, the evaluative process consists not of experiences, but of statements, not of sensations, but of judgements. We encounter evaluative reasoning frequently not only in everyday life, but also in the humanities and the social sciences. Classic examples of such reasoning may be found in Plato's Socratic dialogues.

Evaluative reasoning also forms a pattern, in that every evaluative judgement is logically dependent on some general principle, and general principles (or values, see §8) make it possible to formulate evaluative judgements. I shall call this pattern *the theoretical pattern of evaluations*. The structure of this pattern is determined not only by the content and scope of the given principles, but also by the rules of reasoning adopted within the system. Theoretical patterns do not exist 'independently'; they always have their motivational edge, being connected with motivational patterns in the same way that structure and function are connected in language; but they may and should be distinguished in philosophical analysis.[1]

It may be objected that evaluations form only a part of the statements which go to make up evaluative reasoning; and that, therefore, it is not in fact evaluative reasoning, but reasoning with evaluative components. What is pertinent, however, is that both the necessary original assumptions and the final conclusions are doubtless evaluative. Anyway, a 'purely evaluative' reasoning, would like a set of mathematical formulae, have no bearing on reality.

In the present century philosophers have devoted rather scant attention to evaluative reasoning. This is because contemporary philosophy of value has been dominated by two trends which concur in depreciating the role of intellect in matters of morality and of evaluation in general: by axiological emotivism of various sorts, and

[1] A similar function is performed by K. J. Arrow's distinction between 'tastes' and 'values' of an individual. See his *Social Choice and Individual Values*, 2nd ed. (New York, 1963), p. 18.

by intuitionism, which traces its origins either to H. A. Prichard or to Max Scheler. It is true that Scheler himself, in his writings on the hierarchy of values and on ideal moral types, took the reasoning component into account, but—faithful to his general philosophical position—stressed the pre-eminence of immediate understanding of values.

Perhaps it was not accidental that the possibility of investigating the role of 'reasons' in ethics was postulated by a specialist in the philosophy of science. Since the publication of Stephen Toulmin's *The Place of Reason in Ethics*, the concept of 'good reasons' has frequently been discussed. Although Toulmin conceives of this term as designating, in principle, elements of what I have called the theoretical pattern of evaluations, even his own book is not free from ambiguities. This is due to the fact that the term 'reasons' is itself ambiguous. When philosophers write about 'good reasons', they may have in mind either motivating reasons (that is, motives strong or frequent enough to be recognized as 'good', or—as in Stevenson—'sufficient') or else theoretical reasons (i.e., rational and conscious premises, which we consider well-grounded and usable in a given model of evaluative reasoning).

Kurt Baier seems to have a similar distinction in mind when he writes that 'the question "which type of consideration is superior to which?" is not identical with the question "what sorts of facts tend to move most people or the agent most?"'[1] However, while maintaining rightly that 'it is not true that our ends determine what is a reason for doing something, but, on the contrary, reasons determine what we ought to, and frequently do, aim at',[2] Professor Baier fails to notice that this applies to the motivative, and not to the theoretical, pattern of evaluations. In the theoretical pattern it is the ends which determine what are 'good reasons'. If the aim is to achieve, e.g., an egalitarian society, everything which in a given activity supports and strengthens equality will constitute a 'good reason' for a positive evaluative judgement of this activity.

History, sociology, and psychology supply us with many instances of the theoretical pattern of evaluations playing the role

---

[1] K. Baier, *The Moral Point of View* (Ithaca, N.Y., 1958), p. 99.
[2] Ibid., p. 88.

of a distinct and powerful motivative factor,[1] and also of a factor integrating motivative patterns. Contacts with organized systems of evaluations not only influence human behaviour, but can produce changes in men's needs.[2] It is not even necessary that we fully approve of such a system emotionally or intellectually; our behaviour may be influenced by mere consciousness of the existence of such an orderly scheme of evaluations.

The purpose of the distinction here proposed between motivative and theoretical patterns of evaluations is not only to make more precise the terminology concerning evaluative behaviour and judgements, but also to contribute to a division of labour within axiology conceived as a general science of values. Analysis of theoretical patterns would be basically a task for philosophy. Observation and description of motivational patterns belong primarily to psychology, sociology, and history.

§4. *Descriptive and evaluative statements*

4.1 Evaluation is usually characterized by being contrasted with description. Such an approach is, of course, more sensible than giving abstract definitions; at least it makes clear for what purpose and on what grounds we wish to draw the distinction. However, it is worthwhile to remember that in simply contrasting description and evaluation, without any further specification of what is meant by 'evaluation', we run the risk of conflating two quite different concepts or kinds of things. The point is that both 'description' and 'evaluation' may refer either to certain types of physical and/or mental behaviour, or to the utterances that result from the activities of describing and evaluating. 'Description'-activity takes the form of a person's representing certain objects or events as they appear to him by mentioning their characteristics or indicating them by

---

[1] See, e.g., T. Parsons, E. A. Shils, and J. Olds, 'Values, Motives, and Systems of Action', in Parsons and Shils, eds., *Toward a General Theory of Action*, pp. 159–243.

[2] See, e.g., the influence of the Ancients on the attitudes of men of the Renaissance; the influence of Rousseau on ways of life at the turn of the eighteenth and nineteenth century; M. Weber's and R. H. Tawney's studies on the impact of protestant doctrines on the development of the middle class capitalist morality.

gesture; 'evaluation'-activity may involve purely expressive and non-verbal behaviour such as smiling, frowning, or shrugging. Thus when contrasting description and evaluation we have to make clear whether we are contrasting actions or their verbal products.

Furthermore, it is commonly understood that description issues in the form of sentences (descriptive or declarative statements), while no such requirement seems to hold for the results of evaluation. The product of evaluation, even when it is verbal, does not have to be in the form of a statement but may consist of an exclamation like 'wonderful', 'horrible', 'faugh', 'fie', 'bravo', and so on. Therefore, when contrasting evaluations with descriptions, it is best to do it on their common ground; that is, when both take the form of declarative sentences. Other forms of evaluation, elliptic and expressive, should be compared rather with other elliptic utterances and expressive gestures, like opening one's arms at seeing an old friend, nodding one's head, saying 'silence', 'attention', 'how bright', 'help', 'you bet', and so on.

Such a narrowing of the scope of our comparison—solely to descriptions and evaluations in the form of statements and judgements—helps us to avoid many possible misunderstandings; moreover, it wards off the danger of treating all evaluations *a priori* as expressive and not informative utterances.

4.2 One of the classical statements of the view that there is a clear-cut distinction between description and evaluation is A. J. Ayer's well-known essay 'On the Analysis of Moral Judgements'. Professor Ayer says there that 'There is no procedure of examining the value of the facts, as distinct from examining the facts themselves.'[1] I do not see any reason to disagree with this. But he also writes that 'A valuation is not a description of something very peculiar; it is not a description at all';[2] and this seems to be only a half-truth. It is clear that, unless one is an idealist or an intuitionist, one has to assume that evaluation is not a description of something 'very peculiar', since that something, hidden beyond the facts or within their inaccessible inside, simply does not exist. It is also fairly

---

[1] A. J. Ayer, *Philosophical Essays* (London, 1959), p. 237.
[2] Ibid., p. 242.

obvious that evaluation differs somehow from description. But does it not entail it in some way, is it completely separable? Ayer's theory seems to rest on a particular understanding of description.

His argument runs as follows. Let's suppose that someone has committed a murder. Police investigation has produced certain data: where, when, and how the victim was killed, who were the victim and the killer, what was the relationship in which they stood to one another. We have also gathered information about the motives of the act, the killer's opinions and so on. All these are statements of fact, empirically verifiable or refutable. But, says Ayer,

> when one has said what he did, when one has described the situation in the way that I have outlined, then to add that he was justified, or alternatively that he was not, is not to say any more about what he did; it does not add a further detail to the story. It is for this reason that these ethical predicates are not factual; they do not describe any features of the situation to which they are applied.[1]

At first glance it seems convincing. We may, it is true, voice a few doubts. If it turns out that the act has been committed without premeditation, we shall not call the culprit a 'murderer', only a 'killer'; these terms have different legal meanings and also different evaluative strength. It is also hard to imagine that a premeditated murder committed for the sake of financial gain could be called 'justified'; this predicate seems, at least, to carry negative information about a given fact. These and similar pernickety objections, however, amount to no more than pointing out that evaluations are not pronounced arbitrarily and may be linked to facts. They will do nothing to knock the bottom out of Ayer's argument.

But let us consider two other examples. Let us imagine that our friend Harry has been to an old-fashioned glass factory and now describes how the workers blow glass to make bottles. He tells about the furnace, the big bowl with liquid glass, the pipe, movements of the worker, and so on, and then adds: 'It is easy, I tell you.' In our second story, another friend of ours, Jim, is just back from Switzerland and tells us how he watched a group of climbers going up the Eiger. He describes the climbers' equipment, the

[1] Ibid., pp. 235–6.

weather, the height and steepness of the slope, and so on, and concludes: 'It was dangerous, you know.' In Ayer's terminology, neither Harry nor Jim 'describe' anything in their final remarks: 'easy' and 'dangerous' do not convey any information about the facts, about what has happened. However, neither 'easy' nor 'dangerous' are ethical terms, and probably nobody has ever doubted that they are capable of conveying information. But information of what kind?

We might regard these statements as expressions of feelings or moods. But of what moods or feelings? That would be quite uncertain. Harry did not necessarily intend to boast that he himself could blow the glass; and Jim is perhaps going to try for the north face of the Eiger himself. In any case remarks of this type are commonly understood as referring not to the speakers' emotions but to the objects mentioned. Thus the statements with predicates 'easy' and 'dangerous' are both descriptive, and non-descriptive. The paradox is solved, I believe, by means of clarifying the concept 'description of the features of a situation'. If we understand a situation as an isolated 'case' like the blowing of a glass bottle or a climb up the Eiger, then neither 'easy' nor 'dangerous'—nor, for that matter, a good many other words, like 'safe', 'hazardous', 'facile', etc.—are descriptive.[1] The statements containing them do not tell us anything about entirely isolated situations. If there existed some activity quite impossible to compare with any other, it would be meaningless to call it 'difficult' or 'easy' or 'dangerous'.

But if we assume that a description of a situation may contain information about the relation of this situation to other somehow comparable situations, facts, objects, persons, and so on, a relation of a sort and within a framework implied by the context in which the description is given, then the problem will appear in a different light. 'Easy' will then mean 'not requiring as much effort and skill as other comparable actions'; 'dangerous'—'presenting more pos-

---

[1] Professor Nowell-Smith would perhaps regard these words as 'A-words', i.e., 'Aptness-words', which 'indicate that a certain object has certain properties which are apt to arouse a certain emotion or range of emotions. (*Ethics*, Harmondsworth, Middx., 1954, p. 72). But then what is the 'proper' emotion to be aroused by the words 'easy' or 'dangerous'? Anyway, Nowell-Smith considers A-words descriptive.

sibilities of injury or death than other comparable climbs', or 'other comparable sports', and so forth.

I believe that there is, in this respect, no fundamental difference between evaluative ethical and aesthetic predicates, and words like 'safe', 'easy', and so on.[1] I suppose that Ayer's insistence on finding the object of description *within* a given situation is an unconscious relic of thinking about values as 'intrinsic', somehow hidden inside things or facts evaluated. He has to reject the thesis that evaluations describe something because he understands their possible reference in a way which makes rejection unavoidable. In arguing against the presence of description in evaluative judgements he points out that there is nothing 'valuable' in the evaluated situation itself: no value sticks there like a nail in a wall. He is certainly right; but in fact when assessing a certain action or object we are not talking about that action or object in isolation: we confront and compare them with something else.

The above discussion of Ayer's view may be considered incomplete because the predicates 'easy' and 'dangerous', taken as examples, are sometimes used to evaluate. One might, then, put forward two hypotheses: (1) perhaps only the 'purely ethical' predicates do not describe anything; (2) predicates of the 'easy' and 'dangerous' type describe only when they are not used evaluatively.

To the first hypothesis we reply that to attempt to identify specifically ethical predicates is a hopeless task: the more narrowly and specifically ethical the meaning of a term like 'virtuous', the stronger the tendency to understand it in a technically factual sense; and that even 'typically ethical' terms are sometimes used in obviously descriptive functions.[2]

4.3 Let us now consider the second hypothesis. If in an agreement between employers and a trade union jobs are divided into 'safe' and 'dangerous', or in a war correspondence we read that the Chis

---

[1] The fact that all these words are frequently used as 'persuasives' is of little relevance as, for instance, 'dangerous' may be used both in intention of commanding and of dissuading, depending on the beliefs and temperament of a speaker.

[2] See, e.g., M. Ossowska, *Podstawy nauki o moralności* (Warsaw, 1947), pp. 45–8; G. H. von Wright, *The Varieties of Goodness* (London, 1963), passim.

have 'easily' broken through the defences of the Upsilons, we do not doubt that both terms are used descriptively. When Bill, telling about John's moral predicament, winds up 'but he found an easy way out', or when Don Quixote explains to Sancho Panza that he has to attack a presumed enemy because it will be a dangerous exploit, we do not doubt that here we have to do with evaluative uses. Moreover, in statements of both kinds some factual information, and thus elements of a description, can be identified. For instance, knowing Don Quixote's turn of mind we know what evaluative content the predicate 'dangerous' has for him, but knowing him we are also aware, at least in general, of the kinds of objects or events he will call 'dangerous'.

Between these two poles there can be distinguished many intermediate sorts of usage, for which it would be difficult to determine whether they are descriptive or evaluative. 'It was an easy run', we hear at a Squaw Valley bar, and do not know if it is a positive or a negative assessment, or perhaps a description? 'Easy money' may be a descriptive or an evaluative expression; similarly 'a dangerous work'. However, the issue: description or evaluation is not, and this is what concerns us at the moment, a matter of choice between two mutually exclusive possibilities since, even if we understand, e.g., the statement 'John got rich the easy way' as evaluative, we cannot deny that it contains broadly descriptive information.

The predicates 'easy' and 'dangerous' are sometimes used for purposes of classification, e.g., in tourist guidebooks, where they define types of water- or mountain-routes. Authors of such guides, explaining the principles of classification, and then grouping routes according to these principles, aim apparently at information and description; but the reader may understand their classification as evaluative.

Other classifications possess a more openly estimative character and consist in grading, sometimes measured by the distance from an ideal standard. Since J. O. Urmson's well-known 'On Grading'[1] many papers on this subject have appeared. However, the commonly invoked distinction between 'grading', i.e., a classification according to merits, and 'classifying', i.e., classification according

[1] J. O. Urmson, 'On Grading', *Mind* (1950), pp. 145–69. See also C. A. Baylis, 'Grading, Values, and Choice', *Mind* (1958), pp. 485–501.

to qualities, is far from being a clear-cut one. In fact, this distinction rests either on a difference of aims, or simply on an assessment of what one is to consider a merit, and what a quality. For instance, sorting horses according to their colour is an example of classifying, but not to a captain who looks only for bay remounts for his regiment. We sort eggs according to freshness and size, but in some countries they are also assorted by their shade, because many housewives believe that darker (or, conversely, lighter) eggs have a greater nutritional value. The quality of being brown is for these housewives a merit, perhaps more important than size.

But what does it actually mean to say that 'easy' or 'dangerous' may function as evaluative terms? When do we ascribe to them an evaluative function? Here I can propose only an approximate and tentative answer. It seems that we are inclined to ascribe this function intuitively to predicates, when statements in which they occur serve as arguments or inducements for or against some preference, decision, or choice.

4.4 Generally speaking, the two following methods of distinguishing description from evaluation have been most frequently used in contemporary philosophy: (1) by determining which predicates are characteristically evaluative; (2) by pointing at the emotional contents expressed in evaluative utterances. Owing to G. E. Moore's influence, the 'predicative' method prevailed until the 'thirties; more recently the majority of thinkers have been inclined to believe that evaluation can be distinguished rather on the grounds of the emotional states it expresses.

I shall discuss this more widespread opinion first. It gives rise to many difficulties which are known to at least some of its followers. One of the consequences of this view is that evaluations cannot be uttered with understanding but without a concurrent conviction, i.e., that the element of assertion is necessary. Taken as evaluations statements like 'Van Gogh was a great painter, but I do not like his pictures', or 'John is a scoundrel, but we all adore him', would have to be considered self-contradictory. According to this view we would also have to expect a historian of art, who professionally evaluates works of various periods and styles, to pronounce all judgements with conviction based on his own emotional reactions to those pieces of sculpture, buildings, and canvases. But the task of the art historian is usually conceived as knowing and applying the established criteria of his discipline rather than peddling his personal predilections and talking about his own particular experiences. Let us suppose that the historian in question has never been to Italy and knows Michelangelo's sculptures from photographs only. Should we then refuse to his statements the name of evaluations? Or assume that his statements are in fact quasi-evaluations with just the shape and without the true content of evaluations? (But how can we establish the difference?) Or should we perhaps treat his judgements as assessments of the photographs, or as appraisals of his reconstructions of what Michelangelo's works may be like? This would surely lead to an absurd biographism in our interpretation of scholarly-critical utterances.

The above example indicates that 'emotionalism' in interpreting evaluative judgements turns them into autobiographical confessions, and signals other resulting difficulties. Namely, it we accept this view, the postulate of impartiality will appear impossible to meet, although it is indeed the 'emotionalist' understanding of appraisals which makes this postulate especially important. Moreover, if we can regard a statement as evaluative only when we recognize the emotional state which it expresses, then any utterance whose underlying emotional state is unknown to us cannot be considered evaluative. This also concerns utterances whose authorship is unknown to us, as well as fictitious utterances. Let us imagine that in a deserted house we find a note with the words: 'My neighbour Timotheus Booble is a bad man.' According to the 'emotionalist' theory, to consider this statement evaluative we would have to assume that its author was an emotional antagonist of a Mr. T. Booble. But what if T. Booble never existed? Or never had a neighbour? It really seems more sensible to regard this statement as an evaluation of a fictitious object than to deny its evaluative character altogether.

Thus, to the usual difficulties posed by the interpretation of utterances in natural languages, the 'emotionalist' conception of evaluative statements adds another: a constant necessity to form psychological hypotheses.

In §§12 and 13 I shall try to explain in some detail why I believe

that evaluative judgements should be distinguished from statements expressing emotional states, and also from instructions,
exhortations, and so on. Here, to end this list of objections against
basing the distinction between description and evaluation on the
alleged emotional content of appraisals, I shall add that it is a
psychologistic conception of a pronouncedly irrationalist hue. If
we identify evaluations with expressions of approval or condemna-
tion, elation or contempt, we treat them primarily as utterances
based not on thought but on spontaneous reactions. This may be
justified with regard to evaluations which are not evaluative
judgements, but is very misleading if applied to such maxims as
'Trite are the anxieties of mortals', 'Who lives without madness is
less wise than he supposes', 'Virtue is the only good'. These and
analogous statements are generally understood as evaluative, but it
is hard to see in them only or primarily expressions of emotional
reactions, or symptoms of praising and blaming. In my view,
Kazimierz Ajdukiewicz was correct in pointing out that judgements
of the value of objects are passed both on the grounds of feelings
and on the grounds of reasoning.[1]

Lastly, from its shaping of the very concept of evaluation, the
psychological interpretation of evaluation sides with so-called non-
cognitivism, i.e., the view that evaluative judgements lack cognitive content, prejudging the issue even before it has been raised.

4.5 One appreciates the attractiveness of the psychologistic
position with regard to the description–evaluation issue when one
remembers that it arose as a reaction against idealist and intuitionist
views, which had dominated axiology, and that the 'predicative'
conception was supposed to be the only alternative.

We have already noted that the identification of specifically
ethical predicates is an unpromising task; the same can be said
about all evaluative predicates.[2] First of all, even assuming that the
isolation of evaluative predicates is possible, if we do not wish to
rely solely on intuition we must possess some criterion of classification, and thus are faced with a classic *petitio principii*. And if we
decide that we shall apply the name 'evaluative' to statements in

---

[1] K. Ajdukiewicz, *Język i poznanie*, vol. I (Warsaw, 1960), p. 347.
[2] Ossowska, *Podstawy nauki o moralności*, pp. 44–5, 98–9.

which certain arbitrarily chosen predicates occur, we run into another difficulty, namely, the fact that even 'typically evaluative' predicates sometimes perform obviously descriptive functions ('good price', 'bad temper', 'wrong way', etc.). Aesthetic predicates are in this respect less troublesome, but we cannot rely on them alone and even 'beautifully' may mean simply not more than 'without obstacles'. Finally, many apparently pure descriptive predicates like 'hard', 'elastic', 'slippery', attain in certain contexts an obvious and strong evaluative sense.

Incidentally, it is worth noticing that although the 'predicative' conception has not withstood criticism, it is so simple to employ that many philosophers of value use it as a convenient means of identifying their object of scrutiny.[1]

4.6 Having rejected as hazy and impractical both the 'expressive' and the 'predicative' concepts of evaluation, we must look for some other method of distinguishing descriptive and evaluative statements. Such a method can perhaps be found in an analysis of the role which these types of statements play in a given language.

We know that any proposition can be true or false only within a certain language. Moreover, every expression means something only within the framework of a language to which it is assigned. The rules determining the meaning of words in natural languages are numerous and varied. For instance, the meaning of words which signify colours is linked to the customary classification of visual impressions; the meanings of names referring to weights and dimensions are defined by generally adopted standard units; the meanings of adjectives like 'fast', 'high', 'heavy', are determined by current, usually intuitively grasped, criteria of comparison; the meaning of words like 'devil', 'angel', 'Holy Father', is connected directly or genetically with certain systems of religious beliefs; and so on. It is also clear that within a given national language we have to do with a great many social group languages, and also with a great many situational contexts, causing shifts in the meaning of words and expressions. A 'bath' means a different thing to a photographer than to a metallurgist; a jacket on a book is rather unlike a jacket worn by a jockey; a 'jack' may mean almost anybody or any

---

[1] e.g., Paul Edwards, *The Logic of Moral Discourse* (New York, 1955), p. 141.

semi-mechanical tool, depending on the circumstances; the meaning of 'father' depends on who is addressing whom by this name, and so on.

A national language is, in fact, a conglomerate of coexisting and overlapping group and situational languages. Before we are able to answer the question what a given word, expression, or sentence means, and especially before we wish to decide whether the proposition expressed by that sentence is true or not, we have to determine within the scope of which national, group, and situational language we are going to locate and interpret these words, expressions, and sentences. To quote an old joke: 'I am mad about my flat' means 'I am enthusiastic about my lodgings' in London, and 'I am furious because of a punctured tyre' in New York. 'This is a different proposition' expresses a different proposition when placed within a logical discourse from when it is found in a company's business report. 'Tyrtaeus wrote elegies' and 'Shelley wrote elegies' are two statements which we can verify, but only if we understand the words 'elegy' each time differently, within another conceptual framework. If we applied the first understanding of 'elegy' to the second statement, we would have to deem it false, and vice versa.

That the meaning of words and sentences should be taken as relative to the given group and situational language is, of course, a quite banal thing to say. One has to add, however, that this thesis is usually taken as referring mainly to the relativeness of denotations, i.e., of objects denoted, and not to the relativeness of connotation. In other words, no such attention is paid to the fact that, depending on social group and situation, the same words, while preserving their denotation, may change their connotation. I shall return to this point in §12.3, when discussing the concept of emotive meaning. Also, more attention should be given the fact that group languages differ, not only with regard to the descriptive meaning of words used within their scope, but also with regard to the stock, function, and sense of evaluative terms employed.

Thus, although nobody doubts that in the sentences 'my left heel is broken' the word 'heel' has to be understood differently depending on whether it refers to a part of the foot or a part of a ski, and that 'red' designates a different colour in 'red pine', 'red sunset', and 'red carnations', we keep hearing complaints about the vagueness, imprecision, and even the emptiness of statements containing predicates like 'just', 'noble', 'beautiful', since it is impossible to determine most of their common uses. This is because it has been overlooked that differences in signification of these words may be explained by the fact that they are used within the scopes of diverse 'value-languages', different systems of valuation, with which their functioning is bound up.

It has been amply documented by historians of culture and sociologists that value-systems operative within contemporary European and American societies are greatly diversified. Divergence in evaluations and in the ways of expressing them is much greater today than at the time of our grandfathers, and it is not difficult to identify at least the main causes of this development: disintegration or disappearance of the traditional forms of social life, in many countries the waning of class antagonisms and differences which used to integrate value-systems within given social groups, urbanization, the decline of the influence of religion on *Weltanschauung*. (The more recent phenomenon of 'mass culture' represents an opposite tendency, but only to a limited degree, at the same time reinforcing what is known as social atomization.)

Divergencies in evaluation, formerly coinciding to a large degree with national and social divisions, seen now in sociological perspective, present a blurred and disorderly picture. Therefore I cannot agree with Jerzy Kmita who, in advocating that evaluations be considered within the scopes of respective 'conceptual apparatuses', identifies these 'conceptual apparatuses' simply with group or individual languages.[1] Aside from the problems raised by the concept of 'individual' or 'personal' language (if it can be called language, then only in a different sense from group language), there is the difficulty that in demarcating a given group or personal language we apply criteria other than the coherence, logical or customary, of evaluations as expressed in this language. An individual may operate within several different value-systems—for instance, in subordinating his valuations in one field to religious dogmas, in another to political principles, in another still to prac-

[1] J. Kmita, in *O wartości dzieła sztuki* (Warsaw, 1958), p. 135; also Kmita, 'Wartości i oceny', *Studia Filozoficzne* (1968), No. 1, p. 146.

tical economic considerations. The same observation, *a fortiori*, applies also to social groups and strata. If we identify value-language with group language or individual language, we greatly impede the investigation into the extent to which a set of valuations, employed by the given group or individual, is coherent.

To be an applicable analytic tool, the concept of 'evaluative language', or 'value-language', has to be understood as applying to an ideal model. Evaluative languages are thus to be demarcated on different grounds from national and group languages. Rather, they are like these conceptual systems linked to myths which Lévi-Strauss describes.[1] The division into evaluative languages will, therefore, crisscross the division into national and group languages.

Since various people consider different things good, or aesthetically valuable, and use the same national language to express their thoughts, there is ample opportunity for confusion. It is, therefore, particularly remarkable that in everyday life there are fewer misunderstandings than in the theoretical considerations of philosophy. In any case the conclusion that value-judgements are just expressions of moods or feelings, psychological and personal statements, does not necessary follow from the above socio-cultural observations. If for one person the adjective 'democratic' has a positive, and for another negative, value, there remains a possibility that both of them may be ready to discuss their valuations by means of empirical and rational arguments.

Political terminology provides many examples of terms used in either descriptive, or positive-evaluative, or negative-evaluative functions.[2] Instances, however, may be drawn from other spheres as well: 'romantic' can be a descriptive, or positive-evaluative, or negative-evaluative predicate; 'emotional' may describe or appraise; similarly 'expressive', 'dynamic', 'restrained'. Their evaluative character, and its tone, stems not so much from the personal attitudes of the speakers, as from whole systems of supporting beliefs. And if it is easy to discover instances of statements which may be interpreted both as descriptive and as evaluative, it is

---

[1] C. Lévi-Strauss, 'The Structural Study of Myth', *Journal of American Folklore* (1955), No. 270, pp. 428–44.

[2] See T. D. Weldon, *The Vocabulary of Politics* (Harmondsworth, Middx., 1953), passim.

equally easy to come across identical statements, where one specific utterance of the statement would be evaluative, and another specific utterance would not. In either case the statement, or a given token of it, would belong to a different value-language.

4.7 As the paradigm of evaluative statements philosophers take usually a statement which contains the predicates 'good' or 'beautiful', as the paradigm of descriptive statements a statement with a predicate naming the colour of a physical object. Even apart from the fact that statements about colours are not unambiguous,[1] such juxtapositions also tend to ignore the functions actually performed by such predicates as 'good', 'beautiful', 'bad'. They occur typically in two kinds of context: (1) in shortened, elliptic utterances, and (2) in summings-up and general statements.

In the first context the speaker assumes that the addressee understands which scheme of reference is being applied, i.e., within which value-language the given utterance should be placed. Of course, his value-language may also be of a subjective type: he may say 'A is good' solely on the strength of his personal approval of A. In a context of this kind the information concerning the rules of a given value-language, i.e., primarily the reasons why a given object is called 'good' or 'beautiful', is explicitly stated, usually in sentences which combine descriptions and evaluations and which lead up to the concluding statement. Definition-like statements ('good is, whatever . . .') should be taken as occurring in contexts of type (2); they are nothing else but formulations of the rules of a given value-language.

'John is a good man', 'Poussin was a great painter', are statements of the first type. Their elliptical character is clear from the fact that, if asked what we mean or why we think so, we should try to expound our criteria of goodness and greatness, i.e., explain the rules of our value-language. Instances of the second type can be easily found in literary and art reviews, eulogies, moralistic treatises, Plutarch's *Lives*. ('In his bold purchase deals in the years of bumper harvests and in his restraint in the years of drought,

---

[1] They may be understood as referring either to physical properties of the object, or to visual impressions of the subject, or else to conventional classification of the colour of the object.

John Smith proved himself not only a shrewd merchant but also a good, kindhearted man.')

Evidently, statements of the kind 'this marsh marigold is yellow' represent a quite different type. They are neither elliptical, nor summing-up, nor generalizing.

I shall return again to the concepts of value-languages outlined above in §§8 and 14. It can be summarized in a fairly simple thesis: to understand the context of an evaluative utterance we have to place it not only within the context of a certain national group and situational language, but also, and primarily, within the context of a given value-language.

4.8 In view of what has been said above, in 4.5 and 4.6, there should perhaps be little doubt that it is impossible to distinguish predicates as specifically evaluative on the grounds of their denotation. Should we not, however, try to find a common denominator in their intensional content? J. Kmita believes this to be ill-advised because of 'exceptional vagueness of the notion of intension as applied to expressions in a natural language.'[1] This argument, however, is not quite convincing. We could attempt to make the concept of intension in natural languages more precise by applying it to our concrete needs. By using the concept of connotation postulatively ('we shall call the connotation of an evaluative predicate . . .') we could find out whether the desired level of logical precision is in this way attainable, and, above all, whether it would be feasible to describe by its means some hitherto elusive features of the analysed terms.

This task lies far beyond the scope of the present work, and I shall confine myself to saying that I believe that predicates in evaluative judgements possess a certain common connotative content, an objective connotation which is sometimes concurrent with conventional connotation. The connotation of evaluative predicates includes pointing at the tendency on the part of objects or qualities designated to evoke a certain kind of reaction in people who may be considered the 'referees' of the judgement. Those who understand the value-language to which a given judgement belongs,

[1] J. Kmita, 'Problem wartości logicznej ocen', *Studia Filozoficzne* (1964), No. 1, p. 121.

without, however, subscribing to the value-system expressed in it, can at least visualize the possibility of such a specific reaction; they would be in the situation of a non-believer who knows the principles of Christianity and reads the Gospels.

4.9 Our discussion so far has served to prepare the ground for an inquiry into the moveable line which separates descriptive from evaluative statements by examining the differences between the means used to verify these statements—or, more cautiously, the means used to argue for their truth.

A formal classification of evaluative judgments will be more fully presented in §11. For the moment, we shall characterize them as follows. Like descriptive statements, value-judgements may express both particular and general propositions: 'a stream flows through the meadow', 'there is water in all streams'; 'Roland was a valiant knight', 'brave knights do not fly from the enemy'. General statements may be regarded either as summed-up observations or as defining utterances: 'to have running water in it is a property of a stream'. Similarly with value-judgements: 'no brave knight has fled from the enemy', or, 'an attribute of a brave knight is not to fly from the enemy'. Particular descriptive statements are verifiable by means of observation and by reference to definitions of the concepts used and to the accepted rules of reasoning; general statements can be either tested by experience, as results of empirical inference, or treated as definitions. And the same holds true of evaluative judgements: we can support the particular by means of observation and by reference to accepted meanings of concepts and general evaluative principles; the general we can either test empirically (have there been any brave knights who fled the enemy? and Hector?), or treat as definitions of evaluative concepts.

A slightly complicated but instructive way to compare the methods of argument used in description and in evaluation, is to juxtapose two identical sentences, one of which functions as a descriptive statement, the other as an evaluative judgement. Let us imagine that in 1934 a history professor, describing the French political scene twenty years previously, said: 'Jean Jaurès was a progressive politician' (S_1). At the same time, a journalist, who is an adherent of Charles Maurras, also wrote in an anniversary article: 'Jean Jaurès was a progressive politician' (S_2). Let us further suppose that the truth of both statements is questioned, separately, by two gentlemen, A and B, who agree, respectively, as to the meaning of the predicate 'progressive' in the sense in which it is used by the historian (C_1) and in the sense in which it is used by the journalist of conservative-nationalist persuasions (C_2). The procedure of substantiating both statements S_1 and S_2 would be in such circumstances analogous and would consist of demonstrating that Jaurès's political activity fulfilled the conditions necessary to be classified as progressive in the accepted senses, respectively C_1 and C_2.

Thus, the difference between the two methods of argumentation must lie somewhere else. We find it when we assume that the disputants question the very understanding of the term 'progressive' of, respectively, the historian and the journalist. Defending his statement, the historian-descriptivist would perhaps argue that Jaurès considered himself progressive and was regarded as such by both his followers and his opponents. A might then reply that the equations 'progressive = generally regarded as progressive' and 'progressive = considering himself progressive' are not correct from the scholarly point of view. But, rejoins the historian, in my discipline it is commonly accepted that, if somebody at the turn of the last century proclaimed the necessity of broad social reforms, the abolishment of great private fortunes, introduction of a universal insurance and rent system, and complete political equality of all citizens—these ideas are quite sufficient to qualify him as 'progressive'. But this is not enough, says A. Progress is measured by the degree to which one has liberated oneself from one's entanglement within traditional socio-institutional systems. If somebody believes that the worker should be a patriot and defend his country, he is not progressive, because putting national solidarity over class solidarity cannot be deemed progressive. The historian counters: true, such a priority is characteristic rather of conservative politicians; however, from the point of view of a scientific classification of historical and cultural facts, the concrete role played by the given individual is most important. If his activity as a whole has been directed against the continuation of the socio-political *status quo* and has aimed at a reshaping of the situation into a historically new one (for instance, according to the Marxist criterion, more consistent with the level of the development of forces of production), we historians consider it a sufficient condition for calling such a man 'progressive'. The reference, in one form or another, to the accepted rules of the scientific discipline would end the discussion. (Of course, I do not wish to maintain that scientific concepts, even more obviously factual than 'progressive', are formed without *any* evaluational influence; we talked about that in §1. Nevertheless, the present example represents, in a crude form, an attempt at sticking to description as much as possible.[1])

B's discussion with the journalist would run differently. *B* would attack the idea, expressed in C_2, that progress is a bad thing. The journalist, defending his position, would point at the results of progress, past and probable future, which he considers injurious. We can guess that *B* would believe at least some of these results— e.g., the simplification and greater uniformity of social intercourse —to be beneficial in themselves or preconditions of achieving aims which he deems desirable. If their dispute lasts long enough, they would both invoke certain general principles, saying for example that it is better to think of the salvation of one's soul than of the production of material goods, or that a political system postulating the equality of rights for all citizens is better than a system based on inequality, or that for France it is better to stick to her traditions than to develop industry, and so on.

Let us now look at another pair of statements: (1) John is a tall young man; (2) Paul is a worthy young man. We learn from documents that John was at that time five feet seven inches tall. Somebody, hearing that, objects and says that a young man of this size cannot be considered tall as, according to statistical data, five foot seven is only average for a male Pole born after 1946. True, we answer, but this average is markedly higher than twenty-five years

---

[1] I have presented this fictitious example in some detail to show, among other things, that even on the level of a simple and somewhat naïvely conceived scholarly debate Stevenson's well-known division into 'disagreements in beliefs' and 'disagreements in attitude' is hard to apply. Not only because, as will be shown later, it misleadingly characterizes attitudes, but also because it oversimplifies the problem of 'disagreements in beliefs' which are, after all, based on specific methodological decisions. See Stevenson, *Ethics and Language*, pp. 2–8.

ago, when John was young and stood five feet seven inches. Thus, the statement was true for that time. The important thing is, we would add, not only to place the disputed statement within its proper situational context, but, above all, to establish the criterion of tallness: should it be dictated by current statistics, or perhaps by statistics of the last thirty years (one generation)? We probably leave this decision to demographers.

We learn of Paul that although he himself was living from hand to mouth, he gave to the police a wallet with money in it which he found in the street; that he spends much of his free time looking after his invalid grandmother; that he is always ready to aid his friends. However, we hear also that he frequently bemoans his plight, recounts imaginery afflictions and grievances, and shows his resentment to those who do not sympathize with him. The discussion concerning judgement (2) will focus on the problem of whether magnanimity is a necessary condition of worthiness. Different opinions will be expressed in the form of statements like: 'A worthy man is one who . . .' The basic formulae will sound differently, depending on what position one grants in one's hierarchy of values to worthiness and magnanimity, and depending also on what rank one allots to the various qualities that may enter into the concept of worthiness.

As a final example let us consider the statements: (1) 'The *Expulsion from Paradise* in the Branacci Chapel is a work of Masaccio.' (2) 'The *Expulsion from Paradise* is a beautiful painting.'[1] The verification of statement (1) is a problem of the attribution of a work of art. Such questions are decided by applying various, frequently intersecting, methods of scrutiny, on which there exists a large body of specialized literature. These methods, as all methods of historical research, produce results which are only

---

[1] Statement (1) is, of course, not strictly speaking descriptive, but it still is undoubtedly a statement containing factual information. I am giving it here as an example because most of the factual statements we encounter in everyday life and in scientific literature are neither statements of perception nor statements (in the strict sense) descriptive. As I am unable to consider this question here in any detail, I shall only suggest that statements about perceptual data seem to occupy the opposite pole to value-judgements, while all statements concerning the future are, with respect to their cognitive foundations and possible verification procedures, particularly close to evaluations.

probable in varying degrees. An historian of art will accept statement (1) as true if its contents have been confirmed to a degree regarded as sufficient by methods considered proper to his discipline. Thus, at the basis of the proof there will lie beliefs concerning both efficiency and sufficiency of certain methods of research, in other words, certain beliefs about science.

A discussion concerning (2) should reveal certain evaluative assumptions, which will probably be difficult to formulate precisely, but which will take the form of conditional statements: 'if a painting possesses the characteristics a, b, c, and so on, then we consider it beautiful'; or: 'if a painting evokes the response r, then we consider it beautiful'. Even if the antecedent of the implication had to be different for each particular painting, it would be theoretically possible, although enormously complicated, to formulate the required conditional.

4.10 The above examples do not purport to represent complete models of regular discussions; they are simply supposed to illustrate their most probable and typical course. I shall return to the problem of justification of value judgements in §§9, 15, and 17.

We may now propose that the main difference between descriptive and evaluative statements reveals itself in the choice of arguments used in their support. If one wishes to verify a descriptive statement, one refers in the last resort, to scientific findings and assertions, recognized as binding, and to the rules of scientific procedures. In the case of a simple descriptive statement, uttered in everyday conversation, such final reference is necessary only if the truth of the statement is stubbornly questioned. To prove the truth of propositions like 'there are yellow cowslips there', or 'a stream flows across that meadow', we usually do not need to search very far and ostensive evidence usually suffices. But if somebody maintains that, for instance, the field in question is not a meadow but a peat bog, the water not a stream but a canal, flowers not cowslips but dandelions, and colour not yellow but orange—recourse ultimately to scientific foundations will be necessary. When justifying value-judgements we also fall back on certain general assertions, but they only rarely have a scientific pedigree.[1] Sometimes, as

---

[1] 'Scientific' is used here as a concept historically (and linguistically, see

with Socrates or the scholastic philosophers, we encounter the opinion that it is possible to demonstrate the truth of general rules of ethical evaluation by methods not different from those used in science. Since the eighteenth century, however, it has been almost generally agreed that such general axiological principles cannot be attained by use of normal scientific procedures.

Scientific assertions and rules, which we invoke when substantiating descriptions, vary in character, depending on the discipline upon which the description is based. Sporadically, reasoning may reach the basic premises of the given branch of knowledge. More often, however, it is enough to point at what are the facts established by a particular discipline. Only if the very grounds of a given procedure, or the scientific authority of a whole discipline, or, still more generally, the epistemological or logical basis of the applied method of scrutiny are questioned—only then has one to delve into the first premises and the foundations of models of scientific procedures.

The fact that to vindicate a description it usually suffices to refer to the results of some scientific discipline testifies, above all, to the continual growth of the intellectual and social authority of science in modern times. It does not prove, however, that science itself can be entirely free from deeply hidden valuative undercurrents, which direct its interests and create the difference between its results and any random collection of factual data. Still, the above-mentioned sufficiency of reference indicates that the position of these cardinal evaluative principles (or directives, if we use the language of norms, not of value-judgements) within the structure of scientific thinking is—at least, in contemporary Western science—different from their position within the structure of evaluative thinking.

Preface) relative and signifies 'belonging to a discipline, or a method within a discipline, generally recognized as scientific'. For the fifteenth century the scope of the notion would, then, be different from that in the nineteenth. I entirely agree with Ludovico Geymonat that problems of the philosophy of science, here touched upon, are historical in kind (L. Geymonat, *Filosofia e filosofia della scienza*, Milan, 1960). My remarks concerning the description-evaluation problem should also be understood as historically relative, although this may not always be evident.

Obviously, the role of these cardinal principles (i.e., axiological values, see §8) is different in the exact sciences and in the social sciences and the humanities, especially in view of the lower level of self-consciousness and methodological precision in the latter. Basic decisions made by a physicist (or made for him by his masters) are much farther removed from his everyday, practical scientific work, than the decisions of a humanist scholar, who feels constantly compelled to evaluate, for instance when selecting and classifying the objects of his scrutiny. But it is characteristic for contemporary science to strive, particularly by the application of mathematics, to eliminate evaluation at least from the process of gathering substantial data. The social sciences and humanities seem to be evolving towards a situation such as exists in the natural sciences; namely, to a situation where these cardinal principles provide a general psychological or theoretical impulse only to decisions concerning the object, direction, or method of scrutiny. They do not play an immediate role in the confirmation of statements; rather they permit themselves to remain forgotten as long as the status of a given scientific endeavour is not directly challenged.

In contrast, in value-judgements the reference to cardinal principles is almost immediate, because the contents of these judgements are immediately used for practical human purposes: to arrange preference, direct behaviour, organize experience. In science the practical thrust of cardinal principles manifests itself as well, but it is 'filtered' through scientific procedures, or rather funnelled into methodological postulates. Furthermore, in attempting to substantiate their value-judgements individuals rarely feel authorized to invoke the powerful authority of modern science. However diverse the interests, methods, and conceptual systems of science today may be, particularly of the social sciences and the humanities, their diversity is small in comparison to the enormous variety of cultural types existing today, even within our science-permeated European civilization: cultural types which breed different ideals, models of behaviour, sets of preference.

The position of cardinal principles in relation to value-judgements is also different from the position of the tenets of science which we invoke in verifying descriptive statements. Although these tenets are usually accepted without proof as decisive evidence, the means to substantiate them are known. The procedure will vary in different branches of science, and normally involves checking whether the conditions of a given scientific method are satisfied. The feasibility of founding the cardinal principles in ethics or aesthetics is, however, far from obvious, and agreement about the prospects of such an endeavour seems to be rather remote.

4.11 These summary remarks have, of course, been expressed in the metalanguage of an analytic philosophy of value, not in the language of any given value-system or theory of value. They purport to state the principles on which one could base the demarcation between description and evaluation, and indicate the means of determining to what extent these two spheres overlap. Nothing was said about how the scopes of these spheres are actually shaped. The limits of these scopes are in each case determined by two factors:

(1) the given views on science
(2) the given views on value.

I must explain why I am now talking about scopes and their limits and not, as in §4.9, of a moveable frontier between description and evaluation. This is because, although we can *in abstracto* think about a boundary between description and evaluation, in reality many statements are at the same time both descriptive and evaluative; the fluctuation of scope of these concepts reveals itself frequently in the way that some utterances become evaluative without losing their descriptiveness, and vice versa. Historical change and social variations occur to a large extent in the area where both scopes overlap.

The statement 'Peter is a thief' is both descriptive and evaluative. It contains a proposition that Peter has consciously appropriated an object belonging to somebody else. This proposition can be verified, if necessary, by reference to statements of social and physical science. It is also understood by the majority of people to contain a value-judgement, which can be supported or disputed by reference to particular value-systems and by arguing, for instance, that Peter is not a thief because only hunger made him take a pork chop belonging to Jack. If somebody maintains that the statement 'Peter is a thief' also contains a specific and obvious disrecommendation, my answer to it would be that a similar warning is contained, for example, in the statement: 'The road from A to B through C is longer, narrower, more curvy and bumpy than the road via D.' It should also be noticed that the statement about Peter the thief will not have a negative evaluative content for those who do not recognize the legal and moral rules accepted in a given community, particularly the laws of ownership. To other thieves it may even be a positive recommendation. This statement is indeed analogous to a statement like 'John is a capitalist', which for many a social and indeological group has an unequivocal evaluative slant.

The case of racial classifications seems to be especially instructive. For instance, the statement 'John is a Negro' has a descriptive meaning, verified in terms of external somatic characteristics which form the basis of current definitions of the Negro. For the majority of white inhabitants of Rhodesia or Alabama it has at the same time a distinct evaluative meaning which it does not possess for the inhabitants of Scotland or Maine. Besides, most racists are convinced that their opinions about 'higher' and 'lower' races can be scientifically supported and are not basically different from opinions about longer and shorter routes or passable and impassable mountains. For them, statements with racial predicates are both descriptive and evaluative; for others, who do not share their belief in scientific racism, such statements are only descriptive, but with a different content (e.g., 'Negro' does not have the connotation of 'lazy', 'dirty', 'unreliable', and so on.)

Beliefs concerning the scientific character of particular propositions and whole theories and disciplines are constantly evolving and show great historical variation. For our present problem, the most essential differences are those in beliefs about what can be scientifically established and solved, and what remains beyond the scientists' competence. Of course, I do not wish to suggest that all questions not claimed by science are *eo ipso* evaluative questions. The question, 'What is the average length of the tail of a red dog?' is irrelevant from the point of view of both science and evaluation. What is relevant or irrelevant is, however, an evaluative question, and the answer to it belongs to the 'cardinal principles' mentioned in §4.10. Instances of fluctuation in opinion on these matters can be easily found in any book on the history or methodology of science.

Bentham's psychological utilitarianism, with his 'hedonistic calculus', is a well-known example of a theory purporting to solve in a scientific way the problems of ethical evaluation. Also the mechanistic materialists of the mid-nineteenth century, such as Büchner and Moleschott, claimed that moral issues were reducible to chemico-physiological processes. Some evolutionists, notably T. H. Huxley and up to a point also Herbert Spencer, were convinced that the natural sciences might provide reliable answers to basic ethical questions.

Particular sociological theories concentrate on quite different aspects of social life, establish relationships of diverse types, and open the way to differing kinds of evaluations. Depending on what sort of interrelations one sees among social facts and processes, how one conceives the regularities of social development and of social structures, one regards different statements as scientific. An adherent of sociological psychologism will consider scientifically grounded statements which a behaviourist will reject, a follower of von Wiese's formalist sociology will reject or regard as evaluative many of the statements of a sociologist from the school of Znaniecki, and so on. It is easy to imagine that, depending on the methodological position adopted, opinions on statements concerning human recreational needs, free time, required living space, types of labour, urbanization, and so on, will be quite divergent.

A similar variation obtains in the historical disciplines. The question whether history is nomothetic or idiographic, in itself linked to evaluation in the form of a choice of definite cardinal principles, also influences particular value-judgements, as idiographism gives broader scope to evaluation. Most important, however, are beliefs concerning the possibility and ways of using causal explanation and its scope in history, or the so-called problem of historical determinism. The more causal relations, which can be subsumed under general rules, that we discern in history, the broader is the ground established on which the scopes of description and evaluation may overlap, for instance in the characterization of historical personalities and processes. The more cautious and restrained we are in formulating theses on historical cause–effect relationships, the more limited will be the space given to such overlapping. An extreme case of a total coincidence of both scopes, as in the doctrine and practice of Stalinism, is described by Jan Lutyński.[1]

The broadening and shrinking of scopes in not the work of science only, but frequently results from a mutual influence of scientific beliefs and opinions about values. A typical case is that of the notions of progress and evolution, considered descriptive, descriptive-evaluative, or evaluative, depending on both factors.[2] The disappearance from the penal codes in most civilized countries of punishment for homosexuality has been a result of the development of psychology and physiology. The controversy concerning pornography, carried on with great vigour and for many years, is placed on a quieter and more descriptive ground if we resolve to determine whether pornography, attacked because of the pernicious psychical and social effects, really produces such effects.[3]

The above examples illustrate a shrinking of the scope of evaluation in favour of description. This seems to be a general historical tendency. However, the withdrawal is not always as complete, as in the case of some terms referring to social status (peasant, gentry) or notions connected with religious cults (pious). Acquiring a more prominently descriptive character, an expression may still retain an evaluative tinge, even for people who regard it as basically descriptive (e.g., 'saintly', 'knightly', 'godless', 'sodomite'). This is caused by a certain semantical inertia of language, an inertia which allows for some expressions to retain a part of their old function, although their meaning has been separated from its original evaluative basis.

Finally, we have to mention the great ideological movements, which invest whole groups of concepts with evaluative force: Christianity—humility, sentimentalism—feeling, utilitarianism—

---

[1] J. Lutyński, 'O wartościowaniu i manichejskiej postawie w naukach społecznych', *Kultura i Społeczeństwo* (1958), No. 4, pp. 18–44.

[2] See H. Butterfield, *The Origins of Modern Science* (London, 1950), pp. 191–209.

[3] See J. Frank, 'Obscenity and the Law', in M. Levich, ed., *Aesthetics and the Philosophy of Criticism* (New York, 1963), pp. 418–26.

utility, nationalism—native origin, Romanticism—originality and mystery and so on.

4.12 Let me now sum up the conclusions of this chapter.

'Evaluation' is an ambiguous term; in this book we are to deal primarily with evaluation conceived as a kind of reasoning, and expressed in evaluative judgements.

In §2 and §3 a distinction was introduced between two patterns of evaluation: the motivational, which consists of practical evaluative processes in the psychical life of an individual and in the social life of groups, and the theoretical, which forms the structure of any given system of evaluative reasoning.

In an analysis of the mutual relationships of description and evaluation the concept of a 'value-language' is useful. This is a language in which the meanings of particular expressions, and their interrelations, are subordinated to the general evaluative principles adopted in this language.

While the possibility of formulating a definition of evaluation based on connotative criteria remains open, it is possible to determine that the scopes of the concepts of description and evaluation are changing and fluid. On the one hand the bulk and structure of our scientific knowledge, and on the other the type and reach of our value-systems (minimalist systems, like secular liberalism, cover only a fraction of the scope claimed by more expansive systems, like puritanism), produce mutual overlapping or, on the conversely, shrink the scopes of both description and evaluation.

CHAPTER II

VALUE

§5. *Ambiguity of the term 'value'*

5.1 'Value' is an ambiguous term. Many specific senses (value in music, logic, physics, etc.) cause few misunderstandings precisely because of their specialist narrowness, although one reads critics of the visual arts writing on 'value of colour' and evoking two kinds of association at once, value as worth and value in colour theory. A spectacular instance of such a 'tandem' is Bernard Berenson's famous concept of 'tactile values',[1] which is a fusion of a technical artistic notion concerning a certain type of illusionism in painting and an evaluative notion. Using this blend Berenson tacitly raised a particular painting technique to the exalted level of a standard of judgement.

Both in everyday speech and in philosophical literature 'value' appears in three basic senses, which often overlap and are even more often confused.

(1) Value is what a thing is worth; something translatable into or expressible by some units of measurement or comparison, frequently definable numerically.

(2) Value is a valuable (a) thing or (b) property (quality); something to which valuableness is ascribed.

(3) Value is an idea which makes us consider given objects, qualities, or events as valuable.

This triple meaning is not a peculiarity of English; it exists also, for example, in French and in Polish. Studies on the ambiguity of 'value' are, however, few in number. The most extensive I have come across, the first chapter of L. Lavelle's *Traité des valeurs*, distinguishes only the 'basic meanining' ('l'être justifié et assumé') and 'subsidiary', specialized meanings, and lists a number of

[1] B. Berenson, *The Florentine Painters of the Renaissance* (Boston, Mass., 1896).

synonyms.[1] W. Tatarkiewicz in a paper 'On the Concept of Value' declares a triple ambiguity of the term as used in philosophy:

(A) it designates either a property of a thing, or a thing possessing that property;

(B) it designates either a positive quality, or a quality which may be positive or negative;

(C) it has either a specialized, 'economic' meaning, or a broad, 'philosophical' one.

A comparison of this analysis with the classification proposed above shows that Tatarkiewicz's ambiguity (A) concerns the senses identified here as (2a) and (2b); ambiguity (B) runs through all three senses; and ambiguity (C) puts meaning (1) on one side and meanings (2) and (3) on the other. Tatarkiewicz does not distinguish sense (3).[2]

5.2 Let us look more closely at these three basic meanings.

(1) 'What is the value of this house?' 'Modigliani's canvasses have greatly gained in value.' 'In this herd the black stallion has the highest value.' 'What is the value of *Dubliners* within Joyce's whole work?' These are obvious instances of using 'value' in the first of the senses, differentiated above. It is typical of economic contexts, but it appears in ethical and aesthetic contexts as well: 'Has the life of a genius greater value than the lives of ten average men?' 'Under the impact of Riegl's research the value of late Roman art has grown considerably.' Roman Ingarden, in discussing the second of the five senses he distinguishes uses the word 'value' in this way.[3] A. L. Hilliard's definition of 'value', ascribes to this term a meaning of the type which we are now talking about.[4]

I propose to call this sense of 'value' *quantitative*. 'Value' in this sense is not bound to any particular theory but is a semantically independent unit.

[1] L. Lavelle, *Traité des valeurs*, vol. 1 (Paris, 1951), pp. 3–23.

[2] W. Tatarkiewicz, 'O pojęciu wartości', in *O wartości dzieła sztuki*, pp. 13–14.

[3] 'Uwagi o względności wartości' (1948), in R. Ingarden, *Przeżycie, dzieło, wartość* (Cracow, 1966), pp. 69–70. Also in German: *Erlebnis, Kunstwerk und Wert* (Tübingen, 1969), pp. 81–2.

[4] A. L. Hilliard, *The Forms of Value* (New York, 1950), p. 42.

Utilitarians are inclined to use 'value' in the quantitative sense, although they frequently agglomerate all three senses. In the Marxian concept of economic value the quantitative meaning is obviously, though not solely, present. But economists do not always stick to this meaning; for example, Kenneth J. Arrow, in his excellent book *Social Choice and Individual Values* uses the term 'value' in the third sense distinguished above.

(2) The second meaning has a very wide range, as it may apply both to (a) individual objects or facts (particular acts, works of art), and to (b) certain properties of these (conscious intention, artistic originality). For example, R. Frondizi considers values to be qualities.[1] R. Ingarden, in the study mentioned above, uses the term 'value' mostly in this sense. We find it thus used in Dewey, C. I. Lewis, S. Ossowski, S. Zink.[2] The differentiation of 'mellow' and 'sharp' aesthetic values, proposed by M. Wallis, also employs this meaning,[3] which is probably the most frequently encountered. When we say that somebody's actions possess a great social value, or a given sculpture a high artistic value, or that the value of somebody's behaviour consists in his altruism, or that the value of a novel lies in the wealth of its language—we use the term 'value' in the second sense, which I propose to call *attributive*.

As I have said above, different meanings of 'value' often overlap, i.e., it is possible for the same statement to be interpreted as applying to value in different senses. To make the distinction clearer let us compare: 'The value of this house is £40,000' and 'The value of this house consists in its being the classical example of Kentish Gothic'; 'The social value of his actions is zero' and 'His actions have great social value because they show that self-discipline and perseverance can overcome the handicaps of severe illness.'

Why are these two senses of 'value', (a) as object or fact and (b) as property or quality, banded here together as two species of the same basic meaning (2)? Because with regard to actions and per-

---

[1] R. Frondizi, *What is Value?* (La Salle, Ill., 1963), pp. 5–7.

[2] J. Dewey, 'The Field of Value', in R. Lepley, ed., *Value: A Cooperative Inquiry*, p. 71; C. I. Lewis, *An Analysis of Knowledge and Valuation* (La Salle, Ill., 1947), p. 288; S. Ossowski, *U podstaw estetyki*, 3rd ed. (Warsaw, 1958), p. 159; S. Zink, *The Concepts of Ethics* (London, 1962), pp. 56–60.

[3] M. Wallis, *Przeżycie i wartość* (Cracow, 1968), pp. 185–209.

sonalities the scope of the concept of a property (or quality, or attribute) is unclear and the distinction between attributes and attitudes can be drawn only conventionally. J. Nuttin, following L. Klages, points out that what we call personality characteristics or quality changes depends on the system of values adopted.[1] Moreover, in works of art, the line between objects and their properties is often fluid: are the pattern of colour patches in a painting, and the narrative structure of a novel, properties or objects? What separates these two sub-species of meaning is less important than what they share: which is that value is ascribed (attributed) to properties, objects, or facts.

(3) In everyday speech, as well as in specialized literature—although not too often in philosophy—a third meaning of 'value' is distinguishable. When somebody says that the value of life consists in preserving human dignity, or that the value of lyrical poetry lies in the fact that we experience in reading it a peculiar kind of emotion, he is using the term 'value' of a certain idea, principle, or criterion, which allows us to evaluate particular occurrences, objects, and properties—and, consequently, to ascribe to them value, positive or negative, in sense (2). For instance, if we wish to maintain that the value of a work of art consists in its originality (i.e., that being original is a valuable property), we have to assume that originality is a value. To recognize as valuable acts of charity, we have to consider charity a value; regarding honour as a value makes honourable behaviour valuable.

When Taine describes art's value in human life, he uses the word 'value' in this way.[2] Marx applies it when he declares that work is the source of all economic value, as do the biologist B. Glass, who writes about values as principles of biological selection, and the economist K. J. Arrow, who speaks of individual values as determining the issuing of judgements.[3] Ingarden probably has this third meaning in mind, when he writes on 'cognitive values',[4] or

[1] J. Nuttin, *La Structure de la personnalité* (Paris, 1965), pp. 51–9. See also G. Ryle, *The Concept of Mind* (London, 1949), pp. 116–53.

[2] H. Taine, *La Philosophie de l'art* (Paris, 1865).

[3] B. Glass, *Science and Ethical Values* (Chapel Hill, N.C., 1965), pp. 10–12; K. J. Arrow, *Social Choice and Individual Values*, p. 18.

[4] R. Ingarden, *Przeżycie, dzieło, wartość*, p. 85. In German: *Erlebnis*, p. 99.

when he lists 'positive qualities of values'.[1] Of the same kind are
the examples of values given by Nicholas Rescher in his *Introduction to Value Theory*: economic justice, loyalty, patriotism; and his
concept of 'underlying values' or 'values proper' also belongs to
this category.[2]

This last meaning of 'value' I shall call *axiological*, a conscious
pleonasm to stress that this is the most important and essential
sense for the philosophy of value. This meaning is going to remain
at the centre of our attention.

5.3 The above classification of meanings is intended as provisional
and would certainly require amplification that we cannot enter
upon here. It should, however, suffice as a basis for a few general
remarks.

All three meanings of 'value' have acquired a firm footing and
seem to be equally well embedded in language. Prospects for
eliminating any one of them, or of allotting a special, separate term
to one of them, are meagre. We should, therefore, demand only
that when using the term 'value', philosophers and methodologists
clearly realize and indicate the sense in which they understand it.
Frequent confusion of meanings causes endless misunderstanding. Thus, Max Scheler's argument that if 'values were
relative to life, life itself would have no value,[3] rests on a failure to
distinguish between the attributive and the axiological meanings.
And W. D. Lamont proposes an economic conception of value,
without explaining why demand and its satisfaction has to be the
foundation of value. In expounding his conception he uses 'value'
both in the quantitative and the axiological sense.[4]

The quantitative meaning can appear independently whenever
value is measurable in accordance with commonly accepted
standards, i.e., when applied to commodities, money, and the like,
in economics, medicine, and so on. When a physician says that drug
D is of greater value in the treatment of nephrolitiasis than drug E,

[1] R. Ingarden, *Przeżycie*, p. 129; *Erlebnis*, p. 143.
[2] N. Rescher, *Introduction to Value Theory* (Englewood Cliffs, N.J., 1969),
pp. 4–5, 7, 8.
[3] M. Scheler, *Der Formalismus in der Ethik und die materiale Wertethik*, 2nd
ed. (Halle, 1921), p. 94.
[4] W. D. Lamont, *The Value Judgement* (Edinburgh, 1955).

we may ask by what kinds of research, pharmacological, chemical, etc., the value has been assessed—but it would be nonsensical to ask on what grounds we ascribe value to medicaments in general, because the answer is implied in the tacitly understood definition of a 'medicament'. (When members of some radical Protestant group refuse to grant any value to medical treatment, they usually take 'value' in the third, axiological sense.)

In fields, however, where general agreement concerning aims and standards is absent, both quantitative and attributive values are subordinate to axiological values. To assess the value of particular acts, objects, or qualities, or to ascribe value to kinds of behaviour, products, or properties, we must have at our disposal criteria which make such assessment and ascription possible. An alternative would be to hold that we recognize values immanent in things and actions directly and intuitively. This view can, in turn, be understood in two ways: either as referring to psychical processes which lead to recognizing the value of something, or as concerning the autonomous and independent existence of values. The latter version of such 'intuitionism' is a tenet of axiological realism, while the former is in no way contrary to the thesis of subordination given above. Thus, for instance, a car driver distinguishes at first glance the makes of other vehicles, without analysing their appearance, i.e., their properties, which of course does not mean that he is not employing, unconsciously, some specific criteria. Analogously, hearing that John has jumped into a river and saved a drowning child, we ascribe value to his act not by a process of reasoning involving axiological value, but by simple recognition of value in its attributive sense; circumstances, however can be imagined which would call in doubt the value of John's act, and demonstrate that our initial judgement was tacitly based on acceptance of certain axiological values. For instance he might be a poor swimmer and engaged in an important resistance mission—which would make risking his life and being questioned by the police highly dangerous to his companions.

Similarly, psychologistic critics of art, who write on the 'aesthetic values' of beautiful poems, or sonatas, or paintings, use an ellipsis, because these objects are for them valuable only in so far as they tend to evoke certain specific responses. For them the source of values is in experience, and the tacitly assumed axiological value is constituted by concrete states of mind, either individual or shared by members of some social group, i.e., contemplative life-for-the-moment. When Mieczysław Wallis writes: 'By "aesthetic value" we understand here the capability of evoking in a suitable recipient and within suitable circumstances positive aesthetic experiences'[1]—we are entitled to understand this statement as resting on the assumption that 'positive aesthetic experiences' are what is really valuable and what endows perceived objects with value.

N. Rescher distinguishes the three following 'factors of evaluation': 1. The 'value object', i.e., the object that is being evaluated (and may, in our terminology, be granted attributive value); 2. The 'locus of value'; 3. The 'underlying values'—i.e., axiological values. A locus of value, according to Professor Rescher, is an 'item in respect of which the evaluation proceeds and through which values enter upon the stage'.[2] Is this factor really necessary and separable, as he claims? I do not think so. When we evaluate George as a mean person, or a liar, or a genius, George is both the value object and its locus. In other cases the locus is simply either a particular aspect, or an attributive or axiological value. Rescher's own examples allow for both interpretations. In the statement 'Wiggins' tract is of little value for purposes of cultivation', the expression 'cultivation [of land]' may be taken either as indicating an empirical aspect or as referring to a value, perhaps subsidiary to the value of wealth.

The question of the 'mode of existence' of values, so often discussed, by phenomenologists in particular, looks different with each distinctive meaning of 'value'. Quantitative values (1) exist in the same way as kilograms, pence, coefficients of expansibility, and technical parameters. Attributive values (2) exist in the way that objects (2a) or properties (2b) do. Axiological values exist in the manner of laws and principles of science.

Perhaps because of the tenacity, in ethics and aesthetics, of these idealistic traditions according to which values are autonomous entities, philosophers pay less attention to values in the

[1] M. Wallis, *Przeżycie i wartość*, p. 188.
[2] N. Rescher, *Introduction to Value Theory*, p. 8.

axiological sense than do sociologists, cultural anthropologists, historians, psychologists, and so on. This is a part of the broader phenomenon: the rather loose relationship between value philosophy and contemporary social sciences. Most philosophers adopt an attitude of splendid isolation from the issues and results of sociology, anthropology, and history. An extreme but characteristic example is Professor R. M. Hare, in whose two books on ethics there is not a single mention of any non-philosophical work of scholarship.

A philosopher can attain, independently, only a fairly limited knowledge of man's evaluative behaviour; this knowledge comes mainly through the good offices of specialized disciplines. It seems more prudent to use their results than to rely on one's own guesses, intuitions, and imagination. Nevertheless, many philosophers seem to assume tacitly, as phenomenologists do openly, the existence of a peculiar domain of 'philosophical facts'—and confine themselves to insularly philosophical attitudes and approaches.

§6. *Value as a potentially integrative concept*

Man, as Clyde Kluckhohn said, is an 'evaluating animal'. His behaviour, grounded in valuation, is observed and described by psychologists, historians, sociologists, anthropologists, economists. It would be impossible to present an adequate description of a human individual or group in any of these disciplines without a statement about the individual's or the group's values. This is why 'value' should play the role of a basic concept integrating all disciplines concerned with man and his works.

The concept 'value' supplies a point of convergence for the various specialized social sciences, and is a key concept for the integration with studies in the humanities. Value is potentially a bridging concept which can link together many diverse specialized studies—from the experimental psychology of perception to the analysis of political ideologies, from budget studies in economics to aesthetic theory and philosophy of language, from literature to race riots. . . .[1]

In this situation one could expect the philosophy of value to

[1] 'Summary of Discussion of Cornell Value Study Group', quoted in *Toward a General Theory of Action*, eds. Parsons and Shils, p. 389.

follow Socrates' advice and perform a maieutic function: to be a midwife to children bred by specialized disciplines. Concepts, analysed by philosophers, would come from the fields cultivated by these disciplines, and would be applied and tested within their domains. Philosophers' ideas would be continually confronted with empirical and historical data collected by specialists. Philosophy of value would become a sister of philosophy of science: it would study the knowledge of facts related to valuation.

This has not happened, however, and why it hasn't is a separate problem. Philosophers of value are not totally inactive in the field of integrative efforts, as witness, e.g., two collections of papers and discussions edited by Ray Lepley, or Rescher's recent study.[1] Still, they are not active enough and it is not surprising that their role is taken over by the methodologists of particular branches of science, and that one hears voices demanding that problems of value be removed from the bailiwick of philosophy.[2] It is noteworthy, for instance, that in the Nobel Symposium on value in 1969 philosophers played a minuscule part.[3]

It is quite natural that most research on values and most integrative efforts should have been undertaken by cultural anthropologists and sociologists. The following are a few examples of studies which show a keen consciousness of the need to integrate various branches of knowledge around the concept of value: Ethel M. Albert describes methods used in the social sciences to classify values; D. Bidney discusses the concept of value as applied in modern anthropology: K. J. Arrow integrates economic with ethical and even aesthetic problems; B. Glass draws a parallel between certain problems of ethics and results of biological research; J. Topolski, in his fundamental book on the methodology of history compares the role of evaluation in history and on other disciplines.[4] By and large, the authors of integrative endeavours use the term 'value' in its axiological sense.

[1] R. Lepley (ed.), *Value : A Cooperative Inquiry*, and *The Language of Value*; Rescher, *Introduction to Value Theory*.

[2] A. L. Hilliard, *The Forms of Value*, pp. 7–8, 325.

[3] See *The Place of Value in a World of Facts*, Nobel Symposium 14 (1969), ed. A. Tiselius and S. Nilsson (Stockholm, 1970).

[4] E. M. Albert, 'The Classification of Values', *American Anthropologist*, vol. lviii (1956), pp. 221–48; D. Bidney, 'The Concept of Value in Modern

§7. Some attempts at defining value

7.1 The development of philosophy of value up till the nineteen-thirties has been described by Oskar Kraus.[1] A systematic treatment of newer concepts and tendencies is that of R. S. Hartman.[2] Risieri Frondizi gives a short and useful outline of problems connected with the concept of value; and Nicholas Rescher's compact and lucid *Introduction to Value Theory* contains also an excellent bibliography.

In view of the number and diversity of theories discussed in these books it is all the more striking that many authors of works on the foundations of ethics or aesthetics dispense with any overt definition of value, even in the form of a declaration that they are going to use the term 'value' in such and such a sense. We find no definitions of value in Stevenson's *Ethics and Language*, in Dewey's *Art and Experience*, the books of R. M. Hare, the *Aesthetics* of Monroe Beardsley, or in Toulmin's *The Place of Reason in Ethics*.

Most writers on ethics and aesthetics concern themselves with such problems as the relation of value to 'objective' properties of things, change and durability in values, the objectivity and subjectivity of value, relativity of value, the modes of existence of values, the difference between value-possessing and value-lacking objects, and so on; or they pass directly to investigating, for instance, whether pleasure, usefulness, or harmony are determinants of value; while the concept of value remains for the most part unanalysed and undefined.

Since there is no general agreement as to the designation of 'value', philosophers usually write about values in terms of particular, concrete value-systems. We can put it schematically in this way: philosopher I says that A, B, C, and D are values and deliberates upon this group. Philosopher II, however, maintains that values are A, D, E, and F, and devotes his attention to that set.

Anthropology', in *Anthropology Today*, ed. A. Kroeber (Chicago, 1953), pp. 682–699; Arrow, *Social Choice and Individual Values*; Glass, *Science and Ethical Values*; J. Topolski, *Metodologia historii* (Warsaw, 1968).

[1] O. Kraus, *Die Werttheorien. Geschichte und Kritik* (Brünn, 1937).

[2] R. S. Hartman, 'General Theory of Value', in *Philosophy at the Mid-Century*, ed. R. Klibansky, vol. iii (Florence, 1958), pp. 3–41.

As there is no common ground in the form of a metalinguistic definition—that is, a definition formulated in the metalanguage of an analytic philosophy of values, and not in any particular value-language—it is not clear whether philosophers I and II are talking about (a) various members of the same class W, or (b) objects not belonging to any common class. Even if the former is the case, it is not clear what the differential features of that class are; and, if the latter, then they are talking about different things and any dispute between them will be only verbal.

H. Elzenberg distinguishes the notions of 'perfective' value, and of value which consists in an ability to fulfil desires or to meet needs.[1] Are these subclasses of one class of 'value in general'? Hedonists, utilitarians, and axiological pragmatists use, in principle, only the latter concept, and criticize intuitionists, who use almost exclusively the former. Both the philosopher who maintains that 'values have self-existence' and 'subsist independently of the consciousness of them',[2] and the philosopher who believes that 'value is to be identified with satisfactions such as pleasure and conative achievement'[3] would surely agree that honesty is a value—but would they have the same thing in mind? For each of them honesty would be a value for a different reason, and they would differently define its scope and determinants. Are the 'states of consciousness', that is, 'pleasures of human intercourse' and 'enjoyment of beautiful things', which G. E. Moore, a eudaemonist in disguise, gave as instances of 'the most valuable things',[4] and usefulness (i.e., a specific, empirical relation), which was the value for J. S. Mill, members of one and the same class of values? Do those who write about 'unity in variety' as the basis of aesthetic value have in mind a value of the same category as those who regard intensity of experience evoked by a given object as the basis of aesthetic value? These are simple examples of the ambiguities I have in mind.

Misunderstandings are compounded by the fact that many philosophers do not differentiate between various meanings of the

---

[1] H. Elzenberg, *Wartość i człowiek* (Toruń, 1966), pp. 9–11.
[2] N. Hartmann, *Ethics*, transl. Stanton Coit, vol. i (London, 1932), p. 134.
[3] S. C. Pepper, *The Work of Art* (Bloomongton, Ind., 1955), p. 67.
[4] G. E. Moore, *Principia Ethica* (Cambridge, 1903), p. 188.

term 'value' and mix the attributive, axiological, and quantitative senses. Thus, for instance. S. Zink wonders whether and in what degree value is a property or attribute of particular substances, but the examples given by him show that he has in mind the attributes of virtues (like courage), and of psychical states (like pleasure), as well as of particular objects or events.[1] R. Ingarden writes that 'the value of something seems to be a most complex thing', but in the light of his statements these complexities result, at least partly, from grouping together values as attributes of objects and values as certain, e.g., moral, ideas. The problem of the 'constancy of values' is indeed staggeringly difficult, if these two meanings of 'value' are not distinguished.[2]

Another source of confusion is the pressure of everyday language, in which 'value' and 'valuable' appear in many contexts, expressions, and meanings. Perhaps the most important element in the influence of language is its suggestion of the 'substantiveness' of value. Such expressions as 'lack of value', 'lesser value', 'gaining in value', 'levels of value'. 'experiencing value', 'higher value', and so on, suggest that value is not a kind of attribute, but a kind of substance. It is not easy to shake off this restricting impression.

In languages where terms signifying a value, to evaluate, and to value are etymologically cognate—as in English—the semantic closeness of 'valuable' and 'valued' is frequently perplexing. N. Rescher makes these two neighbouring terms the key to the old problem of the 'objectivity of value' and asks: 'Is something *valuable* because it is *valued* (and so, solely because it is regarded by people in a certain way), or is something *valued*—properly and correctly valued—when it is *valuable*, that is, when it is objectively possessed of certain value-endowing features?' His answer is that both kinds of situation arise. In his terms he is right, but it is his terms which seem questionable. The opposition does not apply to cause–effect relations, but to aspects, and reminds one of the age-less eggs and hen controversy. Gold, for example, is both valued 'because' it is valuable, and valuable 'because' it is valued; and so is everything else.

---

[1] S. Zink, *The Concept of Ethics*, pp. 15–60.
[2] R. Ingarden, *Przeżycie*, pp. 100 and 105–11; *Erlebnis*, pp. 115, 122–8.

To clarify his point, Rescher presents two 'paradigm evaluations': of a postage stamp, 'whose sole value resides in the fact that men wish to own it', and of an apple, 'whose value, quite apart from the fact of being desired, resides in its possession of those characteristics that make for its being nourishing, palatable, hunger-appeasing, etc.'[1] Are these really different in kind rather than in degree? Postage stamps are valued or valuable not simply because there are people who wish to own them; some stamps are rarer than others, some prettier, some are more elaborately printed, have educational content, etc. Any stamp collector would readily explain that there are certain features of stamps which appeal to definite interests. And is the distinction between stamp-collecting and etching-collecting a very sharp one? Conversely, different people consider different characteristics desirable in apples (Friedrich Schiller liked them rotten). Rescher's conclusion: 'There are postage stamp cases, where value derives from being subjectively valued, and apple cases, where value inheres objectively in value-endowing features', is, therefore, futilely dogmatic.

Let us also note that the whole dispute can concern only values in the attributive sense, as it would be plainly nonsensical to ask whether piety or fidelity are valued because valuable, or vice versa; it is also clear that value in the quantitative sense must be valued.

Still, behind this linguistic quibble lies a philosophical problem which we shall return to in §9.1.

7.2. Ambiguities and obscurities in everyday language strengthen the impulse to look for a common essence in all that bears the same name. In the philosophy of values this impulse fosters two characteristic tendencies: (1) a search for a uniform basis of all instances of value and evaluative processes; in modern philosophy the most common form of such axiological monism is probably hedonism; and (2) the insistence on formulating the fundamental questions about value in alternatives: for instance, do values have their source in the objective features of things, or in subjective reactions to them?

When problems are put this way, it is difficult to expect unambiguously sensible answers given in empirically identifiable

---

[1] N. Rescher, *Introduction to Value Theory*, p. 56.

terms. Anti-empirical trends in the philosophy of value are strong, stronger than in any other field of philosophy. At the moment, the most important of these trends is phenomenology, represented in Poland by the late Roman Ingarden and his school. The impressive conceptual subtlety and sensitivity shown in the recognition of even minute terminological ambiguities, so admirable in Ingarden's work, can only rarely be put to use in practical research and analyses, because of the general empirical untestability of his theories. For instance, in the essay already quoted 'What we do not know about values?', Ingarden writes that 'it belongs to the essence of values . . . that there is something in them which inclines us to choose which one of them "ought" to be realized, if it is possible to realize two values, for instance, whose conditions of existence are mutually exclusive.'[1] One would wish it really were so, when one stands before a choice between two incompatible values, like love and duty. In another place he declares that the problem 'in which way there *can exist* values of a certain basic type', and the problem whether 'a certain value, presented to us *in individuo* in an experience and belonging to a certain basic type, *really* exists in the given case, whether it is sufficiently well rooted in the object which seems to be its bearer, or whether we have to do with only a more or less justified appearance of the value being vested in that object', are two separate questions, of which only the first one has been investigated.[2] One would rather think that these problems are really inseparable, and that the former can be investigated only in the light of the latter.

An empiricist should, therefore, aim at translating similar statements into a language which renders them experientially confirmable and try to demonstrate that such translation need not diminish the subtlety of analysis. Thus it seems to me that the problem of the 'obligatoriness of the existence of values'[3] can be more clearly stated in the language of moral psychology, and the issue of the 'independence of the valuability of value'[4] can be presented as the question of connections, or lack of connections, between a given axiological value and other values.

[1] R. Ingarden, *Przeżycie*, p. 97; *Erlebnis*, p. 112.
[2] Ibid., p. 112; *Erlebnis*, p. 129.   [3] Ibid., p. 98; *Erlebnis*, p. 111.
[4] Ibid., pp. 98–100; *Erlebnis*, pp. 111–15.

Apart from the doubts of an epistemological nature, Ingarden's method leads to axiological intuitionism, as it does not provide us with either logical or empirical means of determining what is a value and what is not. We are obliged to accept certain values as given and obvious.

7.3 Attempts have been made to define 'value' independently of any concrete evaluative system but their results do not seem fully satisfactory. The most radical of these attempts was undertaken by R. S. Hartman in his two papers on the definition of value and on evaluative propositions. He put forth a 'purely formal' definition of value, based on a differentiation between a definition and an exposition of the name of a class of objects; a differentiation which leads to his thesis that '"good" is not an ethical, but a logical term'.[1] However, Hartman's definition turns out to be not of value but of a valuable object, and thus a definition, at best, only of 'value' in the attributive sense. An 'approximation' of this definition reads: 'Anything is good (or valuable), if it is what or as it is supposed to be.'[2] But the differentiation itself between what are 'definitional' and 'expositional' properties must, as can be easily shown, rest on evaluation—and in this respect Hartman's argument is enclosed within a vicious circle.

A more cautious, though only very general, suggestion of Tadeusz Czeżowski's is also of a logical nature. In a short article 'What are values?' Professor Czeżowski proposes that 'value' be understood as a modal qualification, referring to a mode of being (*modus entis*) of objects.[3] The proposal sounds interesting, but it does not settle our problem: the question remains, when is it justified (methodologically, or axiologically—and not within a particular value-system) to apply this modal qualification? And only an answer to this question will allow us to formulate a definition of value.

7.4 In twentieth-century axiology particular attention has been attracted by definitions of value formulated by Ralph Barton

[1] R. S. Hartman, 'A Logical Definition of Value', *Journal of Philosophy* (1952), p. 413. See also R. S. Hartman, 'Value Propositions', in R. Lepley, ed., *The Language of Value* (New York, 1957), pp. 197–202.

[2] 'A Logical Definition of Value', p. 413.

[3] T. Czeżowski, *Filozofia na rozdrożu* (Warsaw, 1965), pp. 117–20.

Perry, and genetically linked to a definition proposed by Christian von Ehrenfels and also to a remark of Spinoza's.[1] Perry's relationist conception is the result of tendencies to work out a definition neutral as to specific value-systems, and to attain axiological monism. The faults of Perry's theories seem to result from attempts to combine these two disparate aims.

Perry's first definition of value appears in his most widely known book, *General Theory of Value*: 'Value is thus a specific relation into which things possessing any ontological status whatsoever, whether real or imaginary, may enter with interested subjects.' And in a shortened version: 'value is any object of any interest'.[2]

These definitions have been criticized frequently, although Perry's views have exerted considerable influence. Value cannot be at the same time a relation and an object, and there can be no relation between things where only one thing exists. Perry's definition should, therefore, run perhaps as follows: 'If there is something which constitutes an object of interest, then this object enters into the relation of value with the subject of that interest.' The usefulness of such a definition would depend primarily on our understanding of the term 'interest'.

Perry's thoughts evolved in this direction. In his last book, *Realms of Value*, he gave a new definition, this time not of value but of a valuable thing, and also a definition of 'interest'. These definitions were purported to be both nominal and real.

A thing—any thing—has value, or is valuable, in the original and generic sense when it is the object of an interest—any interest. Or, whatever is object of interest is ipso facto valuable. . . . interest is a train of events determined by expectation of its outcome. Or, a thing is an object of interest when its being expected induces actions looking to its realization or nonrealization.[3]

---

[1] Spinoza, *Ethic*, trans. W. Hale White (Oxford, 1927), p. 116: 'From what has been said it is plain, therefore, that we neither strive for, wish, seek, nor desire anything because we think it to be good, but, on the contrary, we adjudge a thing to be good because we strive for, wish, seek, or desire it.' C. von Ehrenfels, *System der Werttheorie*, vol. i (Leipzig, 1897), p. 165: 'Wert is eine Beziehung zwischen einem Objekte und einem Subjekte, welche ausdrückt, dass das Subjekt entweder tatsächlich begehrt oder doch begehren würde, falls es von dessen Existenz nicht überzeugt wäre.'

[2] R. B. Perry, *General Theory of Value* (Cambridge, Mass., 1926), p. 116.

[3] R. B. Perry, *Realms of Value* (Cambridge, Mass., 1954), pp. 2–3.

The later definition is logically more correct, but its utility is questionable on several counts:

a. Equating value with a valuable thing is an uneconomic reduction of two serviceable concepts to one.

b. It is not easy to say what is the 'object of an interest'. Is it, e.g., the result of an experiment, or rather the confirmation of a hypothesis? In war, the expected actions of the enemy determine our own decisions, but are they the object of interest—or is it, rather, our victory? Many morally important actions elude this conceptual scheme: for instance the behaviour of a prisoner who, in spite of torture, refuses to give the names of his fellow conspirators could be rammed into the compartment of 'interest' only with great difficulty. Such behaviour is not determined by the expected outcome. Kantian 'will obedient to duty' seems to lie outside the scope of this conceptual framework. The notion of 'expectation' is, moreover, not quite clear and it is possible that its definition would, by a circular route, lead to an identification of valuable with valued.

c. It is debatable whether 'interest' in the sense defined by Perry always constitutes the value of a thing. The numerical results of an experiment are not a value, nor is the successful avoidance of an ambush. Is a maniac, whose actions are determined by the expectation of writing a poem in twenty-five cantos producing a value? A positive answer to this question would lead to a kind of axiological solipsism.

d. Aesthetic judgements are difficult to interpret within the scope of Perry's theory. What would constitute a 'train of events' in aesthetic matters? Going to a museum? The process of reading a book? Undoubtedly, when getting acquainted with a work of art we expect to have an aesthetic experience; but when we see a painting or listen to a concerto for the first time, we do not yet know whether this experience will have a positive or a negative quality. We cannot, therefore, be motivated by this quality—whereas it is not the experience itself, but its quality which is or is not aesthetically valuable.

e. Therefore as a definition of attributive value Perry's formula is too broad, for we do not deem valuable all things which are of interest to us. As a definition of axiological value, however, it is too narrow. Values which are not pragmatic in kind, i.e., which do *not* base appraisal on expected results of acts but on conforming to specific rules of conduct irrespective of consequences, slip through the net of Perry's definition. A mother who devotedly nurses her mortally ill child, or a man who fulfils a promise to his dead friend by visiting the grave of his friend's parents, are both behaving in a valuable way, according to some value-systems, although 'interest' does not seem to come into the picture here. J. Hospers is correct in pointing out that Perry's theory is a 'refined version of utilitarianism'.[1] This is why it fits the utilitarian type of value and fails to account for values of the non-utilitarian sort.

A similar approach—soundly empirical, but restricted to what could be called 'practical' values, and *eo ipso* bound to a specific value-system, is represented by Rollo Handy. He takes 'value' 'as equivalent to "what satisfies a need"'.[2] Now if we take 'need' so broadly as to include 'needs' for fidelity, humility, and veracity, the conception resolves into a trivial tautology. On the other hand, if we exclude such values, then the definition turns out to be system-bound.

7.5 Nicholas Rescher, who stresses the fundamentally ideological character of values, proposed the following 'formula': 'A value represents a slogan capable of providing for the rationalization of action by encapsulating a positive attitude toward a purportedly beneficial state of affairs.'[3] There are several elements in this definition which give rise to doubt.

First, the term 'represent' suggests that the 'slogan' in question is more basic than the value itself, which is only a representation; this is probably only a semantic slip, but the relation between 'value' and 'slogan' would have to be clarified. Secondly: what does 'capable' mean? Is it supposed to convey the idea that, even if never used, a slogan potentially capable of serving for the rationalization of an action constitutes a value?

---

[1] J. Hospers, *Human Conduct: An Introduction to the Problems of Ethics* (New York, 1961), pp. 552–3.

[2] R. Handy, *Value Theory and the Behavioral Sciences* (Springfield, Ill., 1969), p. 145.

[3] N. Rescher, *Introduction to Value Theory*, p. 9.

Thirdly, must values be action-bound? What about the values of contemplation, renunciation, self-control? Perhaps they can also be covered by this blanket term, but then 'action' does not mean what it is usually held to mean.

Fourthly, the rather cryptically picturesque term 'encapsulating' allows of several interpretations. Does it mean 'to sum up', or 'to expound', or simply 'to express'? In other words, is the connection between the contents of a value-laden slogan and a 'positive attitude' psychological, or logical?

Fifthly, 'purportedly beneficial state of affairs' introduces a limitation of pragmatic kind. Religion-related values, or the value of charity, are caricatured in such terms. And when a few pages later Rescher quotes samples of values as beauty, novelty, intelligence, equality, where are we to look for 'beneficial states of affairs' linked to these? They surely are not 'encapsulated' in these terms by themselves.

Finally, the formula conspicuously lacks a relativization to given value-systems or value-languages. This is not an oversight, because Rescher, rather unexpectedly, emerges as an absolutist: 'Something cannot be a value for one person and fail to be a value for another. ... If something is a proper value, the considerations which establish this fact will have to be equally compelling for all.'[1] Here speaks not a philosopher of value, but an advocate of a concrete value-system. But 'better life', which he mentions, is not necessarily a better life for men of all cultures and the 'actual welfare of the people' cannot be determined without evaluation, and cannot, therefore, serve as a basis for the objectivity of values.

7.6 Marxist philosophers neglected problems of value for a long time, thanks to which their recent efforts in the field are comparatively unhampered by dogmatic traditions (and references to early Marx are frequent). At the same time, however, their interests remain somewhat rudimentary. Perhaps the best, and certainly a very characteristic work of this genre is that of Oleg Drobnitski.[2] Deliberating upon the nature of values, he introduces a distinction

[1] Ibid., p. 11.
[2] O. G. Drobnitski, *Mir ozshivshikh predmetov. Problema tsennosti i marksistskaya filosofia* (Moscow, 1967).

between value-constituting properties of objects, i.e., values in the attributive sense, and 'valuational representations', or 'values of consciousness', i.e., ideals or values in the axiological sense. The former are objects of needs, interests, and drives; the latter translate these needs, interests and drives into the language of thought and emotion, concepts and images, imagination and judgement. All evaluations, and thus all 'valuational representations', are social in kind.

This line of thought is, however, pursued too briefly to clarify ambiguities, because Drobnitski—like all Marxist axiologists—is perturbed by two major dilemmas: (1) How can values be objective, as demanded by his general philosophical standpoint, and at the same time 'unreal', i.e., not identifiable in objects in any physical sense? (2) How can specific values be certain and binding, as ideology requires, if they cannot be scientifically proven?

Drobnitski's answer to the second question follows the traditional Marxist line: although there is a division between science and evaluation, the values of the working classes are—as Engels suggested in *Anti-Dühring*—a spontaneous realization of the objective logic of historical processes. Therefore, although not scientifically demonstrable, the values of the proletariat (and of the Party) coincide with and foster the laws of historical development.

The answer to the first question Drobnitski finds in contrasting the natural and the social aspects of reality. Man's actions, he says, have a double bearing: he changes nature physically, and at the same time turns natural objects into societal objects. Values reside in things taken as societal objects, physically identical with but different from natural ones.

Drobnitski does not notice that the division into natural and societal objects and facts is a matter of convention and change; that, in fact, what he proposes is not an empirical but an arbitrarily rationalistic opposition. Moreover, the insistence on seeing the source of all values outside individuals and finding it in 'nature' on the one hand and society on the other, produces unnecessary difficulties. For instance, a fairly simple and psychologically easy to explain fact, that men may appreciate objects aesthetically with which they have never been in social contact, drives Drobnitski to look for elaborate and far-fetched rationalizations, e.g., that on the moon man will see 'his own history, his own boundless power over the world'.

Leszek Nowak in his *Foundations of Marxist Axiology* develops a somewhat different and formally sophisticated theory. Like Drobnitski, he takes his cue from the young Marx's idea that values originate in man's social interaction with nature. He also believes that the objective–subjective dilemma is resolved by Marx's concept of an ideal 'social subject', not identifiable with any particular person or an empirical approximation of actually held opinions. To such an ideal social subject are ascribed preferences which 'are necessary for the given social category that he represents if this is to occupy the position within the social structure which it actually occupies'.[1] The question who is supposed to be the arbiter in the matters of 'necessity' and 'actual position' is unfortunately ignored. Viewing the problem from another angle, we have to ask: what are the grounds for assuming that differences in evaluational attitudes correspond to, or at least coincide with, social stratification? To a large extent, although never entirely, they did overlap in times of negligible social mobility, but they certainly do not in the twentieth century. The example of an 'ideal capitalist', as described by Marx, does not clarify the issue, because Marx's concept of 'the capitalist' was based on empirical evidence and defined in economic terms. What the terms are in which the axiological ideal social subject is to be defined remains obscure.[2]

In spite of many ingenious theoretical proposals, Nowak's book would not be very helpful in understanding and analysing evaluative judgements and behaviour—because of its declared anti-empirical bias and pervasive abstractedness. Value is defined in

---

[1] L. Nowak, *U podstaw marksistowskiej aksjologii* (Warsaw, 1974), p. 12.

[2] We seem to be faced by a dilemma: either (1) we insist on defining value-systems in terms of idealized social groups, and find ourselves dangerously far from reality (the danger is both philosophical and political: as history has shown, the consequences of exposing certain evaluations as 'inappropriate' for the given group can be painful); or (2) we deem certain values to be *the* appropriate values of a certain social group, and thus define this group in terms of values held; this, however, closes us within a vicious circle, as it is the ideal social subjects who are supposed to provide the determining characteristics of given value-systems. In fact, both methods have been used.

terms of preference, but it is never explained whether what is meant is preference as shown in actual behaviour or as expressed in judgements. The definition of value itself—as a preferentially arranged set of states of affairs—is too far removed from the accepted usage to be serviceable in interdisciplinary communication. Interpretations, in the proposed terms, of value-systems not directly founded on political considerations would tend to be grotesquely simplified. And one unexpected implication of the theory is its conservatism: who can tell in advance which social subjects are representing the real interests—the real *raison d'être*—of their social categories? That would require a full knowledge of the future, and make choices and preferences virtually automatic. Indeed, Nowak—who gives normative ethics the status of science—rejects as un-Marxist all evaluations not based on already existing preferences.

Thus, although Marx's influence made many axiologists better aware of the social pivots of evaluation, and therefore helped to develop less abstract and more factual tendencies in axiology, the professed Marxists display a signal inclination to anti-empiricism.

§8. *Definition of value*

8.1 One of the aims of my considerations so far has been to show that a prime task on the way to bringing some order into the problems of evaluation is to define 'value' in its axiological sense. On the basis of a definition of axiological value one can formulate definitions of 'value' in the quantitative and attributive senses.

'Value' in the axiological sense belongs in the same semantic category with terms such as 'rule', 'principle', 'law', 'explication', and 'justification'. The meaning of these terms concerns various modes of marshalling and organizing statements or facts.

A definition of axiological value will be different depending on whether value is considered within the framework of theoretical or motivational patterns of evaluation.

In the *theoretical* pattern axiological value is a judgement which constitutes a final justification of other judgements within a given system of evaluations. This judgement ascribes the quality of valuableness to certain objects, properties, or states of affairs. *M is an axiological value if and only if M is a judgement, ascribing the quality of valuableness to objects, properties, or states of affairs, and constituting within the given value-system a final justification of other judgements of the system.*

The judgement called here 'axiological value' is expressed in a sentence, which I shall name the *value-principle*. If, for instance, the judgement ascribing the quality of valuableness to courageous acts is an axiological value, and *eo ipso* constitutes a final justification of evaluations of courageous acts, then the sentence: 'courage is a value' or 'courage is a good', is the value-principle of courage.

It may be objected that the paradoxical formula which makes value a kind of proposition runs counter to common intuitions. Perhaps it does; but I am convinced that values in the axiological sense exist in no other way than as thoughts, which recognize the valuableness of something. However, in order not to offend linguistic habits, I shall generally use the notion of a value-principle—a statement, expressing axiological value.

In the *motivational pattern*, whatever is the strongest or ultimate motivational factor in X's behaviour, overt or mental, is for X an axiological value. The variable 'X' may signify an individual as well as a group.

It is easy to see that for the motivational pattern the definitions of quantitative and attributive values are superfluous, because within this pattern all kinds of values—axiological, quantitative, and attributive—are simply stimuli. (This is another reason why the distinctions between various meanings of 'value' are so frequently blurred.) Thus within the motivational pattern value for a given individual or group may be constituted by the content of a judgement, justifying a positive evaluation of acts of mercy; or the vision of an ideal of social justice; or the sum of money one can get for writing a piece of propaganda; or the fear of physical suffering, and so on.

Within the *theoretical* pattern the definition of *quantitative* value will be: Quantitative value is a quantity of substance, or a measurable degree of a property, to which substance or property the quality of valuableness is attributed within the given system of evaluation W, on the basis of a value-principle.

Attributive value: Any object P or property A, to which a value-principle, accepted within the given system of evaluation W, ascribes the quality of valuableness, is an attributive value or has value in the attributive sense, within this value-system.

Axiological values usually concern states of affairs, such as happiness, honour, equality, but also types of behaviour such as impartiality, honesty, fidelity; formal relations, such as coherence, harmony, and so on. These states of affairs, types of behaviour, attitudes, and formal patterns are frequently called 'ideal', or 'ideals'. Value-principles can contain either names of these ideals, or their descriptions (indefinite descriptions).

Can values be only positive? The proposed definitions do not prejudge the matter, since they allow axiological value-judgements concerning such states of affairs as adversity, shame, harm, such kinds of behaviour as cruelty, egoism, cheating, such formal relations as chaos or disharmony, and so on. Value-principles may occur in both positive or negative forms: 'honesty is good', 'avarice is bad'.

8.2 The above definitions belong, of course, to the so-called 'regulative definitions'.

Among the terms used in the basic definitions, 'justification' in particular requires explication. This term is here used in a descriptive, not an evaluative sense. Its meaning is relative to the given system of evaluation W. Different methods of justification, grounded in different types of reasoning and argumentation, are required, for instance, in intuitionist and in utilitarian systems of evaluation. The proposed definition does not make granting the name 'value' dependent on the type of reasoning in whose justification a given value is used; but it leaves room for the possibility of comparing various types of justification.

The denotation of the concept 'value system', or 'system of evaluation', also has to be explained. Such a system consists of four elements:

(1) An axiological value or interconnected axiological values.

(2) Rules, concerning links, which are considered obligatory, between values (in all three senses).

(3) Criteria of evaluation, i.e., practical directions as to how objects, facts, properties, etc., are to be classified, based on an adopted value-principle or set of value-principles. These criteria

fall into two groups: 1. those which purport to determine whether an object of evaluation really belongs to the class of objects evaluated, e.g., whether a given act resulted from conscious decision and 2. those which purport to determine to what degree an object of evaluation possesses properties considered valuable.

4. Rules of reasoning and argumentation adopted within the system.

Both the content and the structure of systems of valuation are products of historical development. The degree and character of their internal cohesiveness, also, as well as the scope of their practical implementation, are historically conditioned. Instances of value-systems are Epicureanism, Bentham's utilitarianism, various forms of Christian ethics, Marxism, and so on.

The concept of value as defined above is similar to some notions which are linked by the philosophers using them, not with the term 'value', but with other terms. For example, our 'value-principles' resemble the type of statements which C. I. Lewis distinguished as 'analytic statements about the valuable'[1]; also the 'supreme justifying principles', discussed by Herbert Feigl;[2] and the 'basic prescriptions' of John Ladd: 'A basic prescription is one which is used to validate other prescriptions but which is itself not validated within the system.'[3] It is possible to demonstrate that these notions, by whatever terms they are named, are necessarily linked with the concept of value. Max Weber's 'value-axiom' (*Wertaxiom*) also seems to be a concept akin to the one presented above.[4]

§9. *Applicability of the proposed definition*

9.1 The proposed definition of axiological value may possibly become the foundation of an 'adequate theory' (in Petrażycki's terminology)[5] of value, or rather of various adequate theories,

---

[1] C. I. Lewis, *An Analysis of Knowledge and Evaluation*, p. 378.

[2] H. Feigl, '"De Principiis Non Disputandum ...?"', in *Philosophical Analysis*, ed. M. Black (Ithaca, N.Y., 1959, pp. 119–56).

[3] J. Ladd, *The Structure of a Moral Code* (Cambridge, Mass., 1957), p. 152.

[4] M. Weber, *Gesammelte Aufsätze zur Wissenschaftslehre* (Tübingen, 1951), pp. 496–7.

[5] Petrażycki believed that class notions should be shaped according to the

since it prejudges neither the origins of values, nor their empirical attributes nor their ontological status. With this definition, both 'idealistic' and 'materialistic' theories of value can be presented; statements constituting value-principles would sound differently in each theory.

The definition may also be used as a means to identify ideas and beliefs which form the basis of evaluative behaviour, i.e., both evaluative utterances and practical decisions of individuals and groups. Such a 'search for (axiological) values' would consist of looking for propositions, necessary logically to the justification of particular value judgements.

Must values of all types be subscribed to and acted upon consciously? The definition of axiological value in the theoretical pattern covers consciously held values which one could cite in justification of one's judgement. But within the motivational pattern, values do not have to be conscious. Socrates remarked that we are only rarely aware of the motives which direct our behaviour, even in important moral situations.

Many sociologists identify the values of a given group with the values practically implemented by that group. We know, however, that coercion and unawareness of the consequences of one's actions frequently lead individuals and whole societies to behaviour contrary to their deeply felt value-principles and ideals. Nodding dutifully to a tyrant may indicate that the value of one's life is motivationally greater than other values, but it does not prove a deliberate rejection of honesty and civil liberties. Besides, the fact that somebody's overtly unconstrained behaviour agrees with a certain principle does not by itself show that this principle is accepted consciously, or even intuitively, by that person. John never gets furious—simply because he has low blood pressure. Paul does not drink, although he would love to and writes enticing

formula 'C is everything that possesses the property "a"', with 'a' denoting an empirical property, and called such procedure 'the method of forming adequate theories'. See L. Petrażycki, *Wstęp do nauki prawa i moralności* (Warsaw, 1930; 1st ed. 1905); T. Kotarbiński, 'Petrażycki's Concept of Adequate Theorem in the Light of Earlier Related Doctrines', in R. B. Palmer and R. Hamerton-Kelly, eds., *Philomathes. Studies and Essays in the Humanities in Memory of Philip Merlan* (The Hague, 1971), pp. 358–70.

anacreontics—but a stomach ulcer does not permit him to indulge. Peter volunteers for the army, although he is an anti-militarist and not particularly courageous—but he is ashamed to remain a civilian when his friends don smart uniforms. Nor does the violation of some principle necessarily imply its conscious rejection; an absentminded man may take somebody else's pen although he believes in the sanctity of property.

Empirically, all valuable objects are valuable *for somebody*, primarily for given social groups, and whatever of value we encounter in actual practice, is valuable when considered to be such by somebody. In other words: we know no valuable objects apart from objects valued, i.e., considered valuable. However, from the theoretical (logical) point of view things are valuable with respect to and because of definite value-principles. For example: Andrew has rescued a child from a house on fire. His act is empirically valuable, because there are some people who know of it and value it; it is valuable theoretically, because there exists a value-principle which says that it is good to save a human life. This distinction enables us to solve the problem of value of unknown objects: they may be theoretically valuable without being valuable empirically, i.e., without being valued by anybody. Pisanello's frescoes, mentioned in fifteenth-century documents and newly discovered in Mantua, were until recently only theoretically valuable.

The most serious danger presented by descriptions of evaluative systems solely on the grounds of external symptoms. i.e., of behaviour, is ethnocentrism, or culturocentrism: attempting to make descriptions in the categories of *our* value-system, our cultural notions, which may be wholly inadequate to other systems. Cultural anthropologists are especially aware of this risk.[1]

9.2 The proposed definitions codify the distinction between the theoretical and the motivational patterns of evaluation. This differentiation permits us to distinguish psychical and sociopsychological processes, bound up with evaluation, choice, and decision, from the logical structure of evaluative reasoning. For instance, the immediate motive prompting Michael to a decision is an opinion of

[1] See. e.g., F. M. Keesing, *Cultural Anthropology* (New York, 1958), pp. 46-8.

George, whom Michael considers an authority; but when justifying his decision Michael may not refer to George's personal view, but to a principle, of which George has expert understanding. An experienced art critic can often pass his verdict on a painting after just a glimpse; however, he will probably substantiate his judgement invoking some specific criteria, and not necessarily his own experience, on which he has hardly had time to draw. The theoretical–motivational distinction is particularly useful when one has to report on a situation in which there is a discrepancy, or contradiction, between theoretical justifications and actual motives of action—as in the case of Molière's Tartuffe and all hypocrites, or when a certain inculcated motivational scheme lacks theoretical grounding—as in the case of the 'good simpleton' or of people endowed with 'faultless taste' who are unable to justify their evaluations.

9.3 We now have to tackle the problem of values adopted intuitively, not in the form of value-principles, but of certain visions or models, real or mythical. Max Scheler's scale of personal value-types is a well-known instance of 'embodied' values, and modern hero-worship (with the word 'hero' used in a sense broader than Scheler's), or today's mass adulation of television, cinema, and concert hall stars, represents 'personified' values. Such values fall within the scope of our definition. The obstacles encountered in their analysis are no different from the difficulties raised by any attempt at a systematic description of irrational behaviour.

But even irrational justifications are still justifications and can be in some way 'rationalized'—which does not mean that they can be made rational. We can 'rationalize', i.e., justify in a conscious and orderly manner both the cult of money and totemism. Max Weber apparently had this in mind when he wrote that 'One can ... "rationalize" life from most different points of view and in very different directions.'[1]

Value-principles may take various verbal forms. Apart from the primary, 'axiomatic' form, characteristic of theoretically organized systems of evaluation ('it is good to be merciful', 'pleasure is the

[1] M. Weber, *Gesammelte Aufsätze zur Religionssoziologie*, vol. i (Tübingen, 1920), p. 62.

basis of all value', 'truth above all'), they may also take the form of general normative statements ('one should always tell the truth'), or of commands ('always tell the truth'), etc. Although differences in verbal shapes are not without motivational impact, and raise important theoretical issues (see §13), the most important structural factor is their function, which is common to all forms.

Names of virtues often appear in value-principles as shortened descriptions of valuable models of behaviour.

9.4 How do the proposed definitions of value look from the point of view of the perennial debate about the 'relativity of values'? The position is that described by Jerzy Kmita as 'methodological relativism'.[1] Methodological relativism consists in investigating values and value-judgements within their respective value-systems; it does not, however, pronounce on the relativeness or absoluteness of any value in general. This standpoint results from formulating the definition of value in the metalanguage of an analytic philosophy of value, and not in the language of any particular theory or system of evaluation. Seen from this angle, every value is a value with respect to the system in which it occurs. 'Absolute' or 'relative' values may appear within given systems, depending on the content and structure of those systems; the same applies to the notion of things 'valuable in themselves'.

Methodological relativism is, therefore, free from the errors of which Charles L. Stevenson accuses the relativists in his essay 'Relativism and Nonrelativism in the Theory of Value': 'relativism is a type of analysis that takes certain of our terms to be relative terms'; 'a relativistic theory of value is simply one that expands "X is good", for example, into "X is approved by —".'[2] Methodological relativism does not accept this equation but maintains that values are values with respect to a given system, within which we interpret them. (It is interesting to notice that Stevenson appears in his essay to be an absolutist: it follows from his statements that 'X is good' can be understood outside any definite system of reference.)

Every comparative linguist is a methodological relativist, since he investigates meanings of words and forms of inflexion within

---

[1] *O wartości dzieła sztuki*, p. 135.
[2] C. L. Stevenson, *Facts and Values* (New Haven, Conn., 1963), pp. 75, 76.

the context of particular languages. This does not mean, however, that he considers relative sequence of tenses in Latin or rules of declension of ordinal numbers in Polish. A linguist does not say, as Stevenson would seem to suggest: '"laska" is what the Czech regard as love and Poles as a stick', but says: '"laska" means "love" in Czech and "a stick" in Polish'. Similarly, if one says that statements about charity had quite different meanings for early Christians and for their Roman persecutors, and that each time we have to place these statements within their respective evaluative contexts, it does not mean that he considers charity a relative value.

9.5 This book purports to investigate evaluative judgements, not evaluative behaviour; it primarily concerns language and logic, not psychology and history. But proposals concerning analysis of statements would be of meagre import if they could not be put to use in analysis of behaviour. Thus the problem of the usability of our definitions of value in particular sciences, especially in cultural anthropology, sociology, and history of culture, is no less important than the question of their 'impartiality'. The fact that these definitions concur with some pronouncements of methodologists of social sciences, such as Clyde Kluckhohn,[1] seems to testify to a possibility of their practical application. The scope of such applicability must be an object of further study. Even a cursory glance, however, shows that basic statements concerning evaluative behaviour of certain theories in cultural anthropology, such as Malinowski's functionalism, Herskovits's cultural relativism, and L. A. White's neo-evolutionism, can be rendered and interpreted within the framework of analytic concepts here proposed. Similarly, to give but one example of a classical descriptive work, the picture of three civilizations, the Zunis, the Kwakiutls, and the Dobus, presented by Ruth Benedict in her *Patterns of Culture*, would be

[1] Kluckhohn defined value as 'a conception, explicit or implicit, distinctive of an individual or characteristic of a group, of the desirable which influences the selection from available modes, means, and end of action', and in another place: 'that aspect of motivation which is referable to standards, personal or cultural, that do not arise solely out of immediate tensions or immediate situations.' In Parsons and Shils, eds., *Toward a General Theory of Action*, pp. 395 and 424.

even clearer if, before a psychological interpretation of observational data, the behaviour of these three peoples was classified according to their respective values.

The possibility of reinterpreting the views of Karl Mannheim in the light of the proposed definitions also looks interesting. It is true that the founder of the sociology of knowledge once sharply criticized those who attach much importance to 'a choice between values', since he thought that 'The view which holds that all cultural life is an orientation towards objective values is just one more illustration of a typically modern rationalistic disregard for the basic irrational mechanisms which govern man's relation to his world.'[1] However, the crucial word in this statement is 'objective'. If we delete this word, Mannheim's objections will also disappear. In his works he several times took up problems involving evaluation, and wrote, for example: 'The most important role of thought in life consists, however, in providing guidance for conduct when decisions must be made. Every real decision (such as one's evaluation of other persons or how society should be organized) implies a judgement concerning good and evil, concerning the meaning of life and mind.'[2] He even devoted special essays to evaluation.[3] Mannheim so strongly stressed the integrative, meaning-producing role of evaluation in the life of both individuals and society, that it seems that a functional theory of value would constitute a natural supplement of his views.

Finally, the history of culture can be understood as, simply, a history of values: a history of changing theoretical and motivational systems, of ultimate justifications of evaluation. Huizinga's *The Waning of the Middle Ages* is a splendid example of an account of cultural history from the point of view of ideas considered at a given time to be final justifications of human actions.

9.6 In conclusion, let us see how, in the light of the proposed definitions, some commonly used expressions concerning values will appear.

[1] K. Mannheim, *Ideology and Utopia* (London, 1936), p. 82.
[2] Ibid., p. 19.
[3] 'Concrete Examples Concerning the Sociological Nature of Human Valuations', in *Essays on Sociology and Social Psychology* (London, 1953).

'Change of value' may mean either a change of the applied axiological value, after which there follows a change in the appraisal of objects to which this value-principle could refer; or a change in attributive or in quantitative value, following either from a change of axiological value, or else from changes in the object itself (damage, move to another environment, and so on).[1]

'Gaining in value' and 'losing in value' can apply only to quantitative values; 'Acquiring value', and 'loss of value', both to quantitative and attributive values: they may come about in the same way as a change of value.

'Crisis of values' applies, of course, to axiological values only, and signifies a disintegration of coherent theoretical and/or motivational systems of evaluation. Such disintegration, which weakens or destroys the organizing force of a value-principle, can be caused by two factors: either by a breakdown of confidence (for instance, due to loss of religious beliefs) in hitherto accepted axiological values, or else by a discovery of internal discrepancies within a given scheme of justification (e.g., doubts about the possibility of reconciling the principle of individual freedom with the principle of equality of rights for all individuals).

'Creating values' means either forming new axiological values, new value-principles, thanks to which objects previously valueless become valuable (Gothic art at the time of Romanticism, primitive art about 1900), or simply producing or discovering new objects, which are valuable according to already existing value-principles.

'Hierarchy of values' is a particularly ambiguous expression; it may apply to values in all three senses. (1) Axiological value: a hierarchy of values is, within a given system of value-principles, the order of their relative importance, i.e., according to whether and to what degree a given principle rests on and is connected with other principles. Such a hierarchy may, although does not have to be, strictly fixed and rigid within particular systems. (2) Attributive

---

[1] Compare E. Durkheim: 'An object may lose its value or gain a different one without changing its nature; only the ideal need change.' *Sociology and Philosophy*, transl. D. F. Pocock (London, 1953), p. 96. Durkheim's 'ideal' is, roughly, a counterpart of 'axiological value'; he did not, however, notice the difference between a theoretical pattern of evaluations and a pattern of social behaviour, based on acceptance of certain values.

value: a hierarchy of values is a gradation of particular objects, classes of objects, and properties, determined by a value-principle or principles adopted within the given system. Such a hierarchy is only rarely fixed, as it is usually continually modified by increases or decreases in the number of given valuable objects, or in the intensity and frequency of appearance of given properties.[1] (3) Quantitative value: in this sense 'value' is used precisely to facilitate a hierarchical organization of attributive values.

Finally, a few words on the mutual relationship of the terms 'good' and 'value'. A 'good' has usually the same meaning as 'value' in the axiological sense, respected within a given system. 'Goods', however, mean usually the same as 'values' in the attributive sense. 'A good' and 'goods' may only be used in a positive sense, 'value' also in a negative—hence its adaptability to the needs of a meta-language and its popularity among sociologists and cultural anthropologists.

[1] I suppose that differences between an absolutionist and relativist understanding of the hierarchy of values can be reduced to the difference between looking at a hierarchy of values from the point of view of axiological values, and from that of attributive and quantitative values. From the point of view of axiological values, a hierarchy of values within a system of evaluation is usually absolute; from the point of view of attributive and quantitative values it is always relative. A certain obstacle to such an interpretation of this old question may be the fact that Pascal, an 'absolutist', used an eminently 'attributive' terminology.

CHAPTER III

AN ANALYSIS OF EVALUATIVE JUDGEMENT

§10. *A formal classification of evaluative judgements*

10.1 Applying the definition of axiological value given in §8.1 we can define more precisely the concept of evaluative judgement (value-judgement). An evaluative judgement is a proposition, expressed in a declarative sentence, for the validation of which it is necessary, among other things, to invoke directly or indirectly some value-principle. In other words; 'J is a value-judgement' means 'J is a proposition, expressed in a declarative sentence, the truth of which depends on the empirical facts mentioned and on the meaning allotted to the predicate by a given value-principle.' For instance, to validate the judgement 'Henry justly divided his estate between his sons', it has to be shown that Henry indeed has divided his estate between his sons; that this division was done in a way consistent with the accepted descriptive sense of the term 'just' as applied then and there in such cases—e.g., that the first-born received a half of the estate, or that all shares were equal; and, if we recognize this statement as evaluative, that we may invoke a value-principle which ascribes to just deeds the quality of valuableness.

To simplify the terminology, I shall use the terms 'value-judgement' and 'evaluative judgement' as equivalents of 'sentence expressing a value-judgement'.

Value-principles are not evaluative judgements *sensu stricto*. As C. I. Lewis rightly pointed out within the framework of a different conceptual system, value-judgements do not include statements which are 'neither a formulation of value not judgements which experience could verify or confirm. For example, the declaration that pleasure is the good . . . or that nothing is unqualifiedly good but a good will.'[1] Other instances of value-principles are easy to

---

[1] C. I. Lewis, *An Analysis of Knowledge and Evaluation*, p. 378.

give: 'all killing is evil', 'honour is man's most precious possession', 'expression is the most important aesthetic factor in a work of art'.

Obviously, value-principles are not absolute, but function within the scope of concrete evaluative systems. For example, the above maxim about expression will not be recognized within a classical system of aesthetic values; not the statement about honour within ethical systems based on religion.

It is also possible for identical statements to perform the function of either value-principles, or 'ordinary' value-judgements. Thus, for instance, the principle of utility would be for a Puritan ultimately subordinated to the principle of serving God.

10.2 Formally, we may divide evaluative judgements into four categories, differing not only in their kind of subject, but also in the way they are validated:

(1) General, applying to classes of objects, acts, events, and so on; of the form 'all x are valuable'.

(2) Particular, applying to particular objects, acts, events; of the form 'x is valuable'.

(3) General comparative, juxtaposing classes of objects, acts, events; of the form 'all x are more valuable than all y'.

(4) Particular comparative, juxtaposing particular objects; of the form 'x is more valuable than y'.

Let us briefly consider the characteristics of each.

(1) *General value-judgements*. These predicate of the members of a given class of objects, acts, events, qualities, and so on, that they are good, beautiful, noble, or horrid. For instance: 'Spartans are brave', 'gothic cathedrals are beautiful', 'Jesuits are hypocrites', 'Benedictines are diligent.' There are two ways of understanding and, respectively, two ways of substantiating judgements of this type. They may be interpreted as: (a) statements specifying an essential characteristic of the given class of objects, i.e., explications of the intention of a class name. Substantiation then consists in demonstrating that the given objects *are* Spartans, gothic cathedrals, or Jesuits. In Hitler's Germany a 'Nazi' had for a member of the N.S.D.A.P. the connotation of a 'fine fellow', but for a German Jew that of a 'murderous scoundrel'. In other words, for a member

of the N.S.D.A.P. 'a fine fellow' was an explication of the intension of the class name 'Nazi', for a Jew an explication of the said class name was 'murderous scoundrel'. Thus for a member of the N.S.D.A.P. to demonstrate that Heinz was a Nazi meant to substantiate that judgement that Heinz was a fine fellow; for a Jew it meant to substantiate the verdict that Heinz was a murderous scoundrel. Such an interpretative attitude is especially common when national, political, and religious issues are concerned. (b) Statements based on induction: a certain value-principle Z is realized by all (or by a sufficient majority) of observed members of a given class of things. Substantiation consists of demonstrating that this is indeed the case.

(2) *Particular value-judgements.* These are the most common. As they apply to individual objects, events, acts, persons, properties, and so on, their links with definite value-principles and criteria of appraisal are sometimes elusive. That is, it is sometimes difficult to gauge within which system of evaluation the given judgement should be placed. For instance: '*Hamlet* is an excellent play', 'Pericles was an outstanding politician', 'Pater had a bad influence on English prose', are all judgements which may be justified by reference to various principles.

(3) *General comparative judgements.* We juxtapose here two, or more, classes of things, and pronounce members of one of the classes to be more, less, or equally valuable *vis-à-vis* the members of the other compared class or classes: 'Spartans are braver than Corinthians', 'Villagers are less corrupt than townspeople.' As in the case of general value-judgements, the judgements may be interpreted either as juxtaposed explications of the intension of class names, or as statements based on induction. There is a further ambiguity: general comparative value-judgements may be understood either as asserting that *any* member of class X is better than *any* member of class Y, or as asserting that *all* members of class X are cumulatively better than *all* members of class Y.

(4) *Particular evaluative judgements.* Here we juxtapose two, or more, things and declare that they are equally valuable or that one is more or less valuable than the other: 'Cézanne was a better painter than Marquet', 'Dick behaved less honestly than Jack.' It is sometimes hard to decide whether we have to do with a general,

or a particular comparative judgement. 'Tragedy is a higher kind of art than comedy'—is it a comparison of two model objects, or of whole classes of tragedies and comedies?

The last example illustrates another problem frequently encountered in the interpretation of comparative value-judgements. We have to ascertain whether in the evaluation of the objects compared the same set of criteria was used—or was the verdict perhaps reached by means of, and because of, the application of different criteria believed to be appropriate to each object respectively? Indeed, it was in this manner that classical aesthetics proclaimed the superiority of tragedy over comedy; in the same way a good philosophical novel would be valued more highly than a superb whodunit; and, by using different standards, one might evaluate also an honest man who had never had a chance to steal a thing and a man who was brought up among thieves but respected the principles of ownership. Frequently, even after a careful examination of a comparative evaluative judgement, one is unable to discover either a common set of criteria, or any coherent evaluational system, which is applicable to both sides of the comparison and might constitute grounds for the assessment that has been made. If somebody says that Henry IV was a better ruler than Pericles, or that the political system of ancient Athens was more just than that of sixteenth century Poland, we are entitled to consider such judgements to be exercises in empty rhetoric. Devoid of theoretical sense, statements of this kind may still exert motivational pressure; this is why they are frequently found in texts of a political or ideological character.

§11. *The problem of classifying value-judgements from the point of view of their content*

11.1 The formal classification of value-judgements sketched above should be complemented by a classification oriented towards their content. Traditionally philosophers have directed most of their attention to ethical and aesthetic judgements. This is why these two kinds stand out most clearly in our consciousness. But every day we have to do with other types of value-judgements as well: judgements concerning social attitudes, political achievements, intellectual abilities, physical fitness, good manners, academic level, and what have been called 'charientic' judgements (from Greek *charieis*—gracious, pleasant).[1] It is even doubtful if ethical and aesthetic judgements are those most frequently made. It seems that we hear less about men who are good, faithful, and honest than about men who are nice, clever, social, patriotic, stupid, polite, snobbish, or charming.

We try to categorize these various statements and talk about ethical and conative, social and cultural, aesthetic and spiritual values. But we do it groping in the dark, for we cannot be sure whether these categories, grounded in our cultural traditions, are not conditioned by ethnocentrism. Difficulties abound, and not only in borderline cases. For example, if the judgement 'John is honest' is supported by the argument that John, never cheating on weight and giving low-interest credit, strengthens public confidence in merchants as a social group, and the adopted value-principle says that the well-being of merchants is a good, should we not consider this judgement social rather than ethical? It is not easy to say whether 'capricious', 'disorderly', or 'polite' are ethical predicates. For one person 'capricious' is an ethical term, used in judgements to remark upon a failure of patience or humility; for another, it applies to an inability to get along with people, and judgements in which it is used disparagingly are supported by reference to social values, like solidarity or peaceableness.

The above examples suggest that perhaps value-judgements should be classified not according to their predicates, but according to values which serve as their justifications. However, if the former looks a hopeless task, the latter does not seem much more promising. After a thorough analysis of several examples, M. Ossowska concludes that 'delimiting the scope of the concept of morality is a moral issue in itself.'[2] Such demarcation is also influenced by the whole system of ideas of a given thinker, the whole body of beliefs of a given social group. With Epicurus, ethical values can apparently be separated from political ones—but is it possible with Plato? The division will be different in the case of Hegel and in the case of John Stuart Mill. *Mutatis mutandis*, the same can be said about aesthetic values. Demarcation of the frontiers of 'the

---

[1] See P. Classen, '"Charientic" Judgements', *Philosophy* (April 1958).

[2] M. Ossowska, *Socjologia moralności* (Warsaw, 1964), p. 175.

aesthetic' is a matter of both the given system of cultural concepts and the ideas of the theorist: it was different in the case of Croce and in the case of Oswald Külpe. Everyday judgements can be troublesome, too: do 'elegant', or 'charming', express aesthetic appreciation?

The fact that ethical and aesthetic judgements are kept in the foreground of discussion concerning evaluation seems to be characteristic of middle-class philosophy. It belongs to the tradition of the middle classes, and particularly where these are Protestant, to consider moral and aesthetic values strictly personal and individualistic, independent of the social and political ones. The influence of G. E. Moore strengthened these traditions in twentieth century English and American philosophy of value.[1] But both in everyday life and in pronouncements of writers, educators, and politicians, who try to shape the thoughts and behaviour of men, we see a close linking of ethical and aesthetic values with social values like equality, political values like democracy or national solidarity, or 'cultural' values like knowledge or the cult of tradition. The relation of these other kinds of values to the ethical and aesthetic one varies not only with the system of evaluation, but also according to circumstances: cultural and aesthetic values play a more important role at times of peace, at times of war social and political values tend to dominate.

To evaluate the same objects or facts from the point of view of different kinds of values is quite common. The Polish system of giving additional points, at competitive university entrance examinations, to candidates of worker and peasant origin has been hotly disputed. It is evaluated socially: does it help or hinder the implementation of the principle of equality? Culturally: is it favourable to the development of general education and science? Politically: does it make the new intelligentsia ideologically more dependable? Morally: does it not punish innocent people and reward the undeserving? The mutual relations of these aspects may be understood in different ways. Similarly, the memory of the dead, and the care of their graves, so widespread and important in Poland in comparison to many other countries, may be justified by reference

[1] See an article, sharply critical of Moore, by A. W. Levi, 'The Trouble with Ethics: Values, Method, and the Search for Moral Norms', *Mind* (April 1961).

to values moral, or social, or religious, or cultural—or to a conglomerate of all of these.

Examples of systems which consider ethical values supreme are easy to find: stoicism is the classical one; but we have to be on our guard against terminological deception. The motivationally exceptional status of predicates 'ethical' and 'moral' inclines many philosophers, and also propagandists, at least to verbal declarations about the supremacy of ethical values. Thus when, for instance, Brand Blanshard says that 'all political problems are in the end ethical problems',[1] it means something quite different from when M. Fritzhand proclaims the pre-eminence of ethical principles in political life and class welfare.[2] For Blanshard, the essence of ethics is intuitively grounded beliefs about good; Fritzhand has in mind that the best ethic is one grounded in Marxist understanding of concrete social and political situations—he is, in fact, an adherent of a system based ultimately on certain socio-political values.

11.2 The question of the mutual relations and interdependence of different kinds of values has been variously posed and solved, and there seems to be little chance for reconciling divergent and contradictory opinions. The literature concerning the interrelations of ethical and aesthetic values is especially plentiful. Within most systems of evaluation the latter are subordinated to the former, but there are also instances of the inverse order.[3] The belief that both kinds can exist separately is comparatively new. Ancient Greeks blended them together within the ideal of *kalokagathia*; they were indissolubly linked by the Christian philosophers. The 'emancipation' of aesthetic values in the consciousness of the educated public dates since the Italian Renaissance. It went in step with the secularization of European culture. In religious systems aesthetic values are, as a rule, closely bound to ethical ones. The view that there is a division between these two kinds of values gained strength in the nineteenth century and is presently accepted as

---

[1] B. Blanshard, 'Morality and Politics', in *Ethics and Society*, ed. R. T. De George (Garden City, N.Y., 1966), p. 1.

[2] M. Fritzhand, *W kręgu etyki marksistowskiej*, Warszawa, 1966, pp. 120–38.

[3] J. F. Herbart among philosophers; theorists of art are mentioned by M. C. Beardsley, *Aesthetics* (New York, 1958), pp. 561–3 and 583–4.

rather obvious by the so-called enlightened public. This view, however, is also based on evaluation and bound up with the modern tendency to treat aesthetic in isolation from other kinds of experience, or, to put it differently, with the inclination to consider art not as a part of life but as an addition to life. This tendency has been critically discussed, e.g., by Edgar Wind in his lectures *Art and Anarchy*.[1]

The separation of aesthetics from morality is not grounded on evident, empirical distinctions. Quite the contrary, specialists in education have demonstrated that aesthetic interests and issues cannot be isolated within the whole of man's thinking and behaviour, and that there is almost no field of human activity from which they are absent.[2] Historians of culture can list innumerable instances of the intertwining of aesthetic, moral, and ideological factors. In his essay on 'Visual Metaphors of Value in Art' E. H. Gombrich demonstrates that art is permeated by non-aesthetic, mainly moral, values, and that separating them is impossible since their linking reflects the fact that we experience and express them 'synaesthetically'.[3] Therefore when we read that 'aesthetic questions have no bearing on other people's interests, or, we might add, other people's interests on aesthetic questions',[4] we may ask: which interests, and which people? We remember artists who let their families starve, but did not abandon their aesthetic ideals; Botticelli, who under the influence of Savonarola burned some of his paintings; the Nazi persecution of the Bauhaus architects; Zhdanov 'reforming' Soviet music; critics who condemned 'reactionary' abstractionism in the visual arts. In all these cases aesthetic questions turned out to be linked to political and moral ones.

The opinion that in all these cases we have to do with 'mis-

[1] E. Wind, *Art and Anarchy* (London, 1963).

[2] H. Read, *Education through Art* (London, 1934); I. Wojnar, *Esthétique et pédagogique* (Paris, 1962).

[3] E. H. Gombrich, *Meditations on a Hobby Horse* (London, 1963), pp. 12–29.

[4] R. M. Hare, *Freedom and Reason* (Oxford, 1963), p. 145. Professor Hare seems to take his argument as analytic, i.e., as an explication of the concept of 'the aesthetic'. This, however, is to beg the question. Besides, he evidently conceives aesthetic experiences to be so esoteric that there is no possibility of there being any *aesthetic* interests whatsoever.

understandings' and arbitrariness is only partly correct, and is in part itself based on a misunderstanding. It rests on ignoring the structure of certain evaluative systems within which values of a different kind are inseparable. We may criticize and reject these systems, but we cannot deny them internal coherence. Cruel and constricting as they may be, they have their sovereign rights. The recognition of this fact does not, however, commit anyone to consent to an identification of specific aesthetic criteria with ethical standards. Even if we should assume that, according to the rules of certain value systems, a good work of art is one which directs the thought of its viewers to morally elevating objects, or one which helps us to understand our social and political situation, this does not mean that we have also to accept evaluative reasonings like the following: this picture represents a scene from the life of a saint, therefore it is a good picture; or, this novel describes in a way consistent with the conventions of nineteenth century realism the industrialization of a rural district, therefore it is a fine novel. Empirically, we can discern the evidence of links between aesthetic and ethical, and other, values in the influence aesthetic objects have on the public and, what is more difficult to establish, on their makers. Particular forms, themes, and conventions cannot *per se* be considered aesthetically or ethically good or bad.

The problem of the mutual relationship of ethics and aesthetics is analogous to the problem of the relation between, say, sociology and medicine. One might insist on keeping their domains separate, but neither discipline will profit from such obstinacy. One may also consider the findings of medicine to be more important than the findings of sociology, or vice versa. Still, even the closest association of these two disciplines, however understood, does not imply that we cannot and should not recognize a difference in the methods of research and scientific procedures applied in each of them respectively.

11.3 The interdependence of ethical and the other values we have been discussing should be distinguished from another sort of dependence, implied by the Stoics and by Christian philosophers, and succinctly described by W. Tatarkiewicz:

Moral value is, essentially, a derivative value. It arises when we attain, or at least want to attain, a certain good. .... thinking about merit and desiring a merit is not a merit. However, many a man gains merit who did not think of it, but thought about his country, his family, about science or art. Moral value, then, is achieved by the man who strives for other values: these strivings create in him, as an *superadditum*, moral value. This value seems to be higher than others, nevertheless it is derivative.[1]

Against this view two objections may be raised: (1) The 'derivative' character of moral value may be only motivational. In other words, it is postulated that, for a given act to be recognized as, e.g., an act of courage, and not as a display of bravado, its motive should *not* itself be a show of courage. Still, in justifying a positive evaluation of somebody's brave act it is necessary to refer to the value of courage, not to the value of a wardrobe saved from a fire. (2) The view rests on definite assumptions of an evaluative–classificatory kind, which tell us to consider 'moral', and appreciate more highly, spontaneity and altruism, but not dutifulness and the desire for glory.

11.4 From our considerations there should be emerging a picture of actually functioning systems of evaluation: historically shaped and determined intellectual products and motivational complexes whose structure consists only partly in logical connections between value-principles and criteria, and results in part from traditional concurrencies, socio-psychological associations, and the influence of cultural models. These systems may house together values that theoretically have little in common. Racism does not find its foundations in Christian morality, but historically has been its frequent companion. There is surely nothing inherently anti-government in innovative tendencies in the arts, like atonalism in music, but specific historical processes in certain countries have led them to be considered subversive by the authorities and expressive of protest by the artists.

In light of the above, the principle of classification, called 'historical' by R. B. Perry,[2] seems to be the best. It consists in distinguishing historically 'institutionalized' kinds of value. It does

---

[1] W. Tatarkiewicz, *Droga do filozofii* (Warsaw, 1971), p. 316.
[2] R. B. Perry, *General Theory of Value*, pp. 693–4.

not postulate a rigid and universal classification, nor does it result in a sharp demarcating of kinds of value. It simply allows us to talk about concrete, historically operating groups of values, which organize and direct certain domains of human activity, and thus to talk about the ethical, aesthetic, political, conative, values, which may appear in various sets and patterns. These groups form around certain comparatively stable problem centres. The 'locality' of some centres, e.g., the aesthetic, seem to be easier to determine than the position of others. Still, there is little doubt that the problems of pity, fidelity, altruism, avarice, hypocrisy, and cruelty are characteristic moral problems.

And this is the outcome of our inquiry: the question of classifying evaluative judgements with respect to their content has to be answered within the terms of particular value systems, which are connected with different visions of reality, conative attitudes, scientific beliefs, cultural traditions. The demarcation will vary within different systems. Let us add a few examples.

The notorious formula that 'the ends justify the means' is nothing but a general maxim transporting certain given objects of evaluation from the jurisdiction of one type of values to the domain of another. It is most frequently invoked for the purpose of allotting issues which might be considered ethical to the bailiwick of politics. The classical case is that of Machiavelli, who said, for example that the Prince is not obliged to keep his promise since his actions have to be assessed from a political, not from a moral, point of view. To a seventeenth-century American Puritan the statement 'this house is decorated' would express a negative moral opinion, not an aesthetic one. Some people consider the way women dress and the cosmetics they use to be a general cultural matter, while others see it involving a question of morality, or aesthetics. Similarly with the rules of 'good manners': they may be regarded as having a basis in social, or aesthetic, or moral norms, or in various combinations of these. Diligence may be a moral or a social value; and so on.

Within the last decade, numerous court verdicts in the U.S. and Great Britain have demarcated anew, at least in the intention of the judges, the line between ethical and other kinds of evaluation in literature, drama, and the cinema. Novels, plays, or films, which are granted a cultural, conative, or aesthetic importance, are excluded from moral evaluation, as they are accorded the rank of works of art and culture, not of entertainment pieces. Here also 'ends justify means': the profundity of De Sade's ideas is supposed to remove his detailed descriptions of torture and macabre sexual deviations from the reach of ethical evaluation.

An interesting case is that of Walter Pater. In his famous book on the Renaissance he put the pleasures of art and beauty at the peak of human experience and value.[1] The whole sphere of art was for him removed from the authority of moral principles—at least, he has been generally thus understood. But, as frequently happens with pronouncements on these matters, his terminology is sometimes confusing. In his essay on Wordsworth Pater says: 'To treat life in the spirit of art, is to make life a thing in which means and ends are identified: to encourage such treatment, the true moral significance of art and poetry.'[2] In this context, 'the true moral significance' should be interpreted analogously with the expression 'truly beautiful' in the writings of the Puritan preacher Jonathan Edwards, according to whom the 'truly beautiful' were only virtuous Calvinists.

In cases of what Dupréel calls 'implicit morality',[3] the lines between values of various kind may be quite fluid. This is evident when a historian or a cultural anthropologist tries to describe the inpact of a categorized, explicit system of values on an implicit, unwritten system, e.g., in the case of changes in the rules of conduct among the early Germans under the influence of Christianity. Many kinds of behaviour, evaluated by the Christians from a moral point of view, were apparently assessed by the Germans from a socio-ritual angle.

When working out a comparative classification of types of value we are compelled to rely on a half-intuitive form of model concepts. Even if we referred to some general 'knowledge of man and his works', and classified values on the basis of its systematization of human endeavours, we could not escape evaluative entanglements, because such a systematization would inescapably have had to rest on certain value-principles. Thus, as *alles vergängliche*, also

---

[1] W. Pater, *The Renaissance* (London, 1904), p. 239.
[2] W. Pater, *Appreciations* (London, 1907), p. 62.
[3] E. Dupréel, *Traité de morale* (Brussels, 1932), pp. 336–40.

our classifications of types of values are only *ein Gleichnis*—and have to pass their test in practical use.

§12. *Value-judgements and expressions of emotion*

12.1 Theories of evaluative judgement can be summarily divided into two categories: those which accord to value-judgements a cognitive content, and those which refuse them such content. It is customary, especially in American philosophical literature, to call the former category 'cognitive', the latter 'non-cognitive'. There are two kinds of non-cognitivism, both of which have their origin in Hume: emotive and imperative. We shall discuss them in turn.

Both types of non-cognitivism may have two forms: radical and moderate. Radical emotivism has it that value-judgements are nothing but emotive utterances in disguise, or, at least, are translatable into such utterances. For instance, the statement 'A is good' is a disguised form of saying 'I like A'. The classical formulation of this standpoint is that by Carnap:

The supposititious sentences of metaphysics, of the philosophy of values, of ethics (in so far as it is treated as a normative discipline and not as a psycho-sociological investigation of facts) are pseudosentences; they have no logical content, but are only expressions of feeling which in their turn stimulate feelings and volitional tendencies on the part of the hearer.[1]

Moderate emotivists maintain that value-judgements and emotive expressions belong to the same category of utterances. This view was advanced by A. J. Ayer.[2] It was developed into a whole doctrine of 'emotive propositions' by Sören Halldén;[3] its best known and most sophisticated form, in some respects close to radical emotivism, is found in the theories of Charles L. Stevenson. It was he who analysed most fully the similarities between emotive utterances and value-judgements. Characterizing what, in his opinion, binds them together, Stevenson maintained that their common denominator is a peculiar kind of meaning: 'emotive' meaning.

[1] R. Carnap, *Logical Syntax of Language* (London, 1937), p. 278.
[2] A. J. Ayer, *Language, Truth, and Logic* (London, 1946), p. 109.
[3] S. Halldén, *Emotive Propositions* (Stockholm, 1954).

A critical analysis of emotivist theories has to concentrate on three fundamental problems:

(1) Is the translation of value-judgements into utterances expressing emotion always possible and adequate?

(2) Is it possible to distinguish a peculiar 'emotive' meaning of words and expressions?

(3) Does putting value-judgements and emotive utterances into one category really help in axiological scrutiny and in discussions concerning evaluative issues?

12.2 Even if we simplify matters limiting our attention to those expressions of emotion which have the form of statements about the emotion of a given person or group towards a certain object (see §5.1), the external difference between these statements and value-judgements concerning the same objects will be obvious. 'John is a good man' is a statement about John; 'I like John', or 'I approve of John', are statements about myself. To identify both kinds of statements solves the problem of their verification: for a psychologist, equipped with a dispositional definition of 'liking' or 'approving', the truth of statements about the emotions of a given person is, theoretically, fairly simple to discover.

This, however, seems to be the only advantage of such an identification. By and large, the awareness of a difference between the two kinds of utterances is quite manifest. The class of good people is ordinarily distinguished from the class of people liked. The latter tends to be broader, and we do not regard all those liked as good. Therefore, although some people are inclined to think that Edward's statement 'John is a good man' implies that Edward likes John, hardly anyone would conclude that Edward's statement 'I like John' implies that Edward considers John a good man.

The difference may also be seen in the ways both kinds of statements are used as premises in evaluative reasoning. The fact that one likes something, that something gives one pleasure, arouses sympathy, is attractive, and so on, is frequently invoked as an argument for appraising that thing as valuable: 'I feel safe in his company, he must be a good man'; 'The audience enjoys itself—the best proof that the show is good.' But the fact that something is valuable, or even that one considers something valuable, is rather infrequently mentioned as the reason why one likes this thing, derives pleasure from it, considers it nice, and so on. Quite the contrary: such a line of argument is often looked down at as snobbish or servile; more common are statements of the sort: 'I know he is a worthy man, but I do not like him'; 'I know it is a great novel, but I am bored by it.'

In other words, statements expressing emotions, or informing about felt emotions, function sometimes as value-principles. A man, for whom his own pleasure or disgust are final justifications of his value-judgements, is an egocentric hedonist. In philosophical theories non-egocentric hedonism is more frequently encountered —it identifies all value with somebody's pleasure. It is that value-constituting role, performed sometimes by emotive utterances, which—coupled with hedonistic and utilitarian traditions—has contributed to the fact that some contemporary philosophers equate emotive utterances and value-judgements. Thus, R. M. Hare writes that '"I approve of A" is merely a more complicated and circumlocutory way of saying "A is right".'[1] This opinion is analogous to saying that the statements 'The United Kingdom has 60 million inhabitants' and 'I believe that the U.K. has 60 million inhabitants' have the same meaning. To say 'A is right' is to say that A meets some criterion of rightness; but to say 'I approve of A' is to say something about one's mind, to express one's positive attitude towards A; the connection between that attitude and any criteria of rightness is another matter.

Philosophers who, like Stevenson in his 'first pattern of analysis', translate 'this is good' as 'I approve of this; do so as well',[2] have some difficulty in explaining statements of the form 'X is good, but I do not like X'. This paradox can, I think, be interpreted in two ways: (1) as analogous to the statement 'X is not red, it is scarlet', i.e., as a tacit contrasting of two different criteria; (2) as an elliptic utterance purporting to suggest that X is good according to certain standards which the speaker recognizes but with which he is unable to agree emotionally. Rather than as self-contradictory, such a statement may be treated as analogous to the example cited by L. Susan Stebbing:

[1] R. M. Hare, *The Language of Morals* (Oxford, 1952), p. 6.
[2] Stevenson, *Ethics and Language*, pp. 96-7.

I might say: 'This is a good hammer, but I am not using it well.' Such a judgement implies that the object called 'this hammer' is well devised for its purpose of hitting nails on the head, but that the person using it is not very successful in hitting the nail.[1]

Similar, although more complex and serious, situations are frequent in cases of emotional and evaluational crises. Stephen Dedalus in Joyce's *Portrait of the Artist as a Young Man* knows that he is breaking the rules of Catholic morality to which he subscribes both intellectually and emotionally, but at the same time he feels powerfully attracted by forbidden kinds of behaviour. If we equate 'this is good' with 'I approve of this', or 'I like this', we make a clear description of such situations well-nigh impossible.[2]

Evaluating an object and pronouncing a value-judgement do not have to be bound up with feeling any particular emotion towards this object. This is especially evident in the case of objects distant in time or space. 'A cruel, shameful slaughter', we say about the extermination of the Albigenses in Toulouse, but the emotion, if any, with which we utter that, is weaker than the emotion with which we appraise the behaviour of a naughty child at the table.

Here we come to the next difficulty presented by radical emotivism: how to identify *the* emotions which are equivalents or counterparts of value-judgements? If evaluative judgements are expressions of emotion, which emotions do they express? Are these emotions also revealed in some other way? Is an emotion expressed in a value-judgement in some way different from an emotion unexpressed? No emotivist has so far clearly answered these questions.[3] Observation of human behaviour seems to indicate that the connections between emotions and judgements are rather loose, even accidental: an intense emotion does not have to be accompanied by an extreme judgement; the same judgement may appear in various emotional situations; similar emotional states may accompany different evaluations.

In the face of all these difficulties radical emotivism is now only

---

[1] L. S. Stebbing, *Thinking to Some Purpose* (Harmondsworth, 1945), p. 42.

[2] The issue is further complicated by the fact that 'approve' has connotations intellectual rather than emotive; 'approving of something' and 'liking something' are far from being synonymous.

[3] See A. MacIntyre, *A Short History of Ethics* (New York, 1966), p. 260.

rarely upheld. The tendency to put value-judgements and emotive utterances into one category is, however, quite frequently encountered. What is supposed to be their common characteristic? 'Emotiveness'—but variously understood.

12.3 The term 'emotive' was introduced to contemporary philosophical vocabulary in 1923 by Ogden and Richards in *The Meaning of Meaning*. They wrote about 'emotive functions', 'emotive use', and 'emotive effects'.[1] But the propensity to treat evaluative statements as emotive originates with Hume, who asserted that

The rules of morality ... are not conclusions of our reason. ... it is evident our passions, volitions and actions, are not susceptible of any such [reasoned] agreement or disagreement; being original facts and realities, complete in themselves, and implying no reference to other passions, volitions, and actions.[2]

The salient elements of his views were belief in the existence of a separable class of 'moral sentiments', and the opinion that man's reason is motivationally 'inert, and can never either prevent or produce any action of affection'.[3] Hume's ethical concerns were, in fact, mainly psychological. Convinced that a logically correct choice of values is unattainable for the human mind, if only because emotions cannot be true or false, he was interested in the ways and means of influencing behaviour. His legacy to the philosophy of value consists, apart from emotivism, in depreciating the role of intellect in formulating and analysing evaluations.

Twentieth-century emotivists did not uphold Hume's theory of moral sentiments, nor did they follow the route, indicated by Ogden and Richards, of analysing the emotive functions of value-judgements. Instead, there has been developed a theory of 'emotive meaning', which is supposed to mark out evaluative statements, or evaluative predicates, and to form a link between them and expressions of emotion. That theory was for the first time and most fully

[1] C. K. Ogden and I. A. Richards, *The Meaning of Meaning* (New York, 1938), pp. 10, 125, 234–6.
[2] D. Hume, *A Treatise of Human Nature* (Everyman's Library, London, 1911), vol. ii, p. 167.
[3] Ibid.

expounded by Charles L. Stevenson, who distinguished 'independent' and 'dependent' emotive meaning, i.e., meaning unconnected and connected with description.[1]

The concept of emotive meaning gives rise to many objections. First, emotions do not form a homogeneous class of psychological facts.[2] Depending on whether we have in mind emotions–moods, emotions–propensities, or emotions–feelings, the term 'emotive meaning' will apply to something different. To say that an evaluative predicate, or a value-judgement, 'means' a mood or a propensity, is not the same as to say that it 'means' an affection or a feeling —although the same words may be connected with any of these.

More importantly, it is far from clear on what grounds 'emotive meaning' is to be identified.[3] Is it constituted by the expressive function of a term or statement, and by the intention of the speaker, or by the evocative impact, by the reactions of the hearers, or by both these factors together? It would seem that it is the functional element of the reaction which is essential, but Stevenson himself warns that 'changes in emotional *effects*' do not necessarily represent a change in 'emotive *meaning*'.[4] As Stevenson's pragmatic–dispositional conception of meaning relies upon the actual use of words, his warning leads to a methodological confusion, since how else, if not through effects, can we recognize 'a dispositional property of the sign', i.e., its meaning? The difficulties, arising from the expressive–evocative ambiguity, are compounded by the very fact of Stevenson's use of a thoroughly causal theory of meaning with its far-fetched psychological implications.[5]

Under the influence of pragmatism, Stevenson blurs the distinction between the meaning and the use of a word. In fact, his theory of meaning is much better suited to cover the expressive–evocative *function* of utterances than to account for the *meaning* of signs which only occasionally perform such functions. Therefore, if we ask: what is the *genus proximum* within which 'emotive' constitutes a

---

[1] Stevenson, *Ethics and Language*, pp. 43–6, 71–9.

[2] G. Ryle, *The Concept of Mind*, pp. 83–115.

[3] For a detailed discussion see J. O. Urmson, *The Emotive Theory of Ethics* (London, 1968), pp. 24–37.   [4] Stevenson, *Ethics and Language*, p. 278.

[5] For a brief criticism of this theory see M. Black, *The Labyrinth of Language* (Harmondsworth, 1968), pp. 215–20.

differentia specifica, the answer will not be easy to find, because to establish the meaning (non-emotive) of terms such as 'abstract', 'older', 'voluntaristic', or 'synchromatic' on the basis of any 'processes in the hearer' would be a rather unpromising task.

Furthermore, declaring emotions to be causes and/or effects of a certain kind of meaning, characteristic of evaluative predicates and utterances, involves presenting these emotions as isolable and final reasons for expressing and/or accepting evaluations. Indeed, the reason for John saying 'Dick behaved brutishly', or 'Ted is an honest man', may be that John feels revolted by Dick's behaviour and is favourably impressed by Ted's character. But these emotions must also have their causes, they are not without reasons of their own. John feels enraged because he saw Dick behaving in a certain way, and is impressed because he heard about Ted's concrete actions. And in expressing his judgements he is not simply giving vent to his emotions (which he may or may not feel, *pace* Stevenson), but also indicating *why* he feels them.

Inadequate as Stevenson's theory may be, the subject itself, i.e., the 'emotiveness' of some terms or utterances, asks for an interpretation. Let us begin with a few simple observations. Virtually any word of everyday language may have an emotive function; names of places—Culloden, Gettysburg, Waterloo—offer a striking example. Conversely, no word performs always the same emotive function, nor even preserves the same degree of 'emotionality'. 'Good', the emotivists' favoured term, is frequently no more emotive than, e.g., 'fit for use'. Or take 'horrifying' in the statement: 'Smith reported his horrifying experience.'

It is possible to use and understand words without feeling anything about their meaning: as one does not have to see red to understand and use 'red', or ever to have felt the thirst for power to communicate about it, so one may use terms like 'noble' or 'avaricious' without either feeling or evoking any emotion. Moreover, we commonly use 'emotional' words to express and convey feelings or moods, or attitudes, contrary to the ones with which these words are linked in dictionaries. It is as if we used the emotional 'charge' of these words, but for purposes different from that for which this suits them. 'You beastly brute', 'you scoundrel', may be terms of endearment; and then there are those stories about generals who would address their favoured troops as 'bastards' and 'sons of bitches', but reprimand soldiers by calling them 'nice boys' and 'excellent guys'.

In his critical discussion of the concept of emotive meaning, Professor Black gives as an example of the contrast between an 'informative' and an 'emotive' utterance the following pair of statements:

'The train is arriving now.'
'That damned bone-shaker is just creeping in.'[1]

The latter plainly says something more than the former, and differently. What *is* the difference? The second statement is emotionally slanted but, in fact, we cannot be absolutely sure which way. Apparently against the train, but is it unimaginable that the speaker, a great admirer of old trains, is expressing his favourable emotion by a kind of sentimental irony, designed to deflect a possibly adverse reaction of the hearers and evince from them a benevolent feeling? As we all know, 'inverted commas', or simply ironical, use of evaluative terms is a subtle means of expression–evocation, subtler and frequently more dependable than straightforward praise or blame.

To illustrate the point, Black's example may be supplemented by other versions of the statements, for instance: 'That masterpiece of railway engineering is just rolling in.' On the face of it, all words here have a distinctly 'positive' emotional tinge; but it is easy to imagine the statement being used sarcastically.

What do these versions have in common? Their denotation, of course. But how can we describe, without knowing the intention of the particular speaker and the reaction of the particular hearers, i.e., without knowing the psychological functions of the statements in any *given* case, the difference between them? I think they may be accounted for in terms of the *connotation* of the words used. The difference between the sets of propositions which can be truly asserted about 'arriving' and 'creeping in', about 'train', 'bone-shaker', and 'masterpiece of railway engineering'—these differences fully explain the divergence of meaning between the words denoting these actions and objects.

[1] Ibid., pp. 140–1.

Apart from that, however, we have the element of emotive functions, to whose service these words have been and may be harnessed. These functions are twofold: expressive, and evocative, or motivational.[1] The relation of these functions to meaning is not very close, as we have seen: we may have the same meaning and divergent functions, and the same functions may be performed by words of divergent meaning. These two should not, therefore, be confused, although it is, of course, true that if a word comes to be used with an emotive function frequently enough this may influence its connotation; e.g., 'beggar', 'heavenly', 'superman'.

12.4 Stevenson and, following him, some other emotivists, distinguish two types of disagreement: 'disagreement in belief' and 'disagreement in attitude'. The latter type is supposed to be characteristic of ethical and generally axiological conflicts. This classification constitutes one more ground for maintaining that there is a fundamental kinship between value-judgements and emotive utterances, which sets them apart from other kinds of utterances.

It is not clear whether Stevenson's differentiation of the two types of disagreements is to be understood as factual, i.e., as a report on two different types of situation, or as methodological, as a means to facilitate interpretation of evaluative behaviour. Introducing the distinction, Stevenson presents it at first as a methodological one; he admits that he does not contrast two mutually exclusive possibilities and that beliefs cannot be separated from attitudes.[2] Then, however, he seems to treat beliefs and attitudes as empirically distinct and isolable facts. His apparent lack of consistency apart, we have to analyse his classification in turn under the two headings, factual and methodological.

Dividing disagreements into 'disagreements in belief' and 'disagreements in attitude' looks a little like dividing certain objects

---

[1] This is a different classification from that of M. C. Beardsley (*Aesthetics*, p. 118), who contrasts emotional purport (capacity to affect the hearer's feelings) and emotional import (capacity to convey information about the speaker's feelings); there the expressive function has been left out. J. L. Austin's gently hypostatizing concepts of 'illocutionary' and 'perlocutionary' forces' (J. L. Austin, *How to Do Things with Words*, Oxford, 1962) apply only to 'performative utterances'; the first covers both expressive and evocative aspects. [2] Stevenson, *Ethics and Language*, pp. 5–6.

into apples and orchard trees. 'Belief' is a term applied to psychological dispositions and signifying a readiness to certain specific kinds of mental and physical behaviour; 'attitude', also a dispositional term, does not signify any concrete tendency, readiness, or capability, and may apply to any set of psychical dispositions, a consistency between beliefs and behaviour included. Besides, the content of a belief may be true or false; an attitude may be rational (based on intellectual beliefs) or irrational (based on habit, mood, emotion). If we understand 'attitude' broadly, it appears that no agreement in belief is possible without an initial agreement in attitude. Moreover, the very concept of 'disagreement', as used by Stevenson, is unclear; as John Hospers has pointed out, 'disagreement in belief' and 'disagreement in attitude' are not two subclasses of 'disagreement', but types of behaviour, distinguished in either case by means of different criteria.[1]

In fact, Stevenson's division seems to boil down to a difference between rational and irrational attitudes. A. Sesonske was right in remarking that a 'rational settlement is possible in every case in which the disputants agree to settle the dispute rationally, and if they do not do so this indicates nothing about the possibility of rational settlement.'[2] It is possible to discuss irrationally most rational subjects, like genetics, or rationally most irrational ones, like preferring blondes to brunettes. In one word, the irrationality of the attitudes of the dissenting persons does not prove the irrationality of the object of their dispute, nor vice versa.

Thus understood as a description of two different types of situation Stevenson's division is untenable. As a methodological concept, however, it insinuates an irrationalist vision of moral disagreements, and of ethics in general. As Hume treated emotions and passions as *given*, so Stevenson seems to treat attitudes as elementary and homogeneous determinants of action. But emotions and passions are not simple sensations but processes, which one can influence, which can be shaped and changed; similarly, attitudes are not closed and final psychical wholes.

Men quite often do indeed base their positions in matters moral,

[1] J. Hospers, *Human Conduct*, pp. 567-8.
[2] A. Sesonske, 'On the Skepticism of "Ethics and Language"', *Journal of Philosophy*, No. 20 (1953), p. 611.

political, or aesthetic, on unanalysed and uncontrolled inclinations, wishes, longings, and so on. But they do not *always* do so; and an ethical or generally evaluational discussion, limited to opposing such unreflective attitudes, would surely be regarded as foolish. At the very least, in situations where there are established standards of judgement, a settlement of a 'disagreement in attitude' is possible by means analogous to settling a 'disagreement in belief'. In the case of a conflict of irrational attitudes one normally tries to identify their sources and attempts to solve the issue by way of an analysis of its origins. Irrational attitudes, like emotions, do not spring up without reasons. It may turn out that the conflict has arisen because of ignorance or misunderstanding. At any rate, since attitudes are not simple, isolable psychical facts, it does not seem sensible to classify them without paying attention to their grounds. Not attitudes as such, but attitudes in connection with their foundations, are morally, and generally axiologically, meaningful. If Jack hates Jim, it is important to find out whether he does it because Jim is a scoundrel or because he is a Negro. As Max Black said, focusing attention upon the irrational aspects of ethical communication and leaving ethical issues 'to be resolved by the interplay of generated emotive influence seems not merely inconvenient but almost mischievous'.[1]

As I mentioned above, the irrationalism of the emotivists has its source in Hume, who considered mind a captive of passions: 'Reason is, and ought only to be, the slave of the passions, and can never pretend to any other office than to serve and obey them.'[2] His ethical interests were, therefore, almost exclusively with the motivational pattern of evaluation; they were one-sided and left a one-sided legacy. Its general assessment depends on the answer to a simple question: does rational argument influence our behaviour? This seems to be today largely a rhetorical question, because such a possibility has been conclusively confirmed by psychologists, and even by recent research in neurophysiology.[3]

---

[1] M. Black, *Language and Philosophy* (Ithaca, N.Y., 1949), p. 220.

[2] Hume, *Treatise*, ii, 127.

[3] I owe this information to Professor Bogusław Żernicki of the Institute of Experimental Biology, Warsaw.

12.5 To interpret '*x* is good' as equivalent to 'I like *x*' or 'I approve of *x*' is to apply a certain normative methodology, as such an interpretation does not follow from an analysis of the meaning of these statements. Therefore, our answers to the questions posed at the beginning of this section are:

(1) The translation of value-judgements into utterances, expressing emotions, is not always possible and is never adequate.

(2) The identification of a special 'emotive' meaning of terms and statements seems neither useful nor possible.

(3) Banding together value-judgements and expressions of emotion into one class of utterances rests on dubious methodological assumptions and obfuscates rather than clarifies the problems of evaluation.

§13. *Value-judgements, commands, and prescriptions*

13.1 Imperativism, and its offshoot, prescriptivism, may be considered related forms of emotivism. Imperativism originated with Stevenson himself, who equated the emotional impact of a value-judgement with that of an exhortation or persuasion. However, for the sake of systematic clarity and with no attempt at a historical presentation, I shall here discuss separately the arguments of those who identify value-judgements with imperatives (radical emotivists) and those who maintain that value-judgements are a sort of prescriptive statements, or that they imply imperatives or normative statements (moderate imperativists and prescriptivists).

The radical version, upheld only in the fervour of polemic, was most succinctly expressed also by Carnap: 'But actually a value statement is nothing else than a command in a misleading grammatical form.'[1] It is fairly obvious that this view could not be defended as it was stated. Later imperativists, of whom R. M. Hare is the best known and most influential, assert more cautiously that logical analysis of evaluative judgements reveals the presence of an imperative or a norm as its fundamental and characteristic component: 'We are therefore clearly entitled to say that the moral judgement entails the imperative.'[2]

[1] R. Carnap, *Philosophy and Logical Syntax* (London, 1935), p. 24.
[2] Hare, *Language of Morals*, p. 172.

The views of moderate imperativists may be interpreted in two ways: (1) The essence of evaluation is prescription or commanding; value-judgements are a kind of normative–commendatory utterances. (2) Value-judgements entail commendatory–prescriptive statements. We shall analyse these two interpretations in turn.

13.2 'The language of morals is one sort of prescriptive language' writes Professor Hare in the first paragraph of his first book.[1] Further on he explains several times that to interpret all evaluation otherwise than as commands is a misunderstanding. Hare considers his thesis true by definition.[2] However, we are entitled to ask if the decision to adopt such a definition is methodologically sound.

Let us begin with doubts of a logical nature. Evaluative judgements are, in their grammatical form, declarative sentences. Commands, norms, and prescriptions do not belong to this category. W. Dubislav has shown conclusively that between declarative and imperative statements there is a sharp logical distinction.[3] The thesis that they belong to the same logical, or (as Hare employs the concept of 'commendatory meaning'), semantic class could be defended only on the grounds that they perform the same functions. Such functional identity could possibly outweigh structural differences.

Do value-judgements perform the same functions as norms and commands? Value-principles indeed appear sometimes to play the role of general norms of conduct. 'Killing is evil' can function as equivalent to the command 'do not kill', or the norm 'one ought not to kill'. Usually, however, men react differently to statements of the type 'John is a good man' and of the type 'you ought to behave like John does'; differently to 'it is wrong to do A' and to 'don't do A'. A simple act of introspection will show, beyond doubt I believe, that our intentions also vary when we utter the above statements: we wish to communicate not quite the same type of content, to evoke not quite the same kind of response.

One may accept a value-principle, or a value-judgement, but hesitate when faced with a prescription which seems analogous to

[1] Ibid., p. 11.   [2] Ibid., p. 164.
[3] W. Dubislav, 'Zur Unbegründbarkeit der Forderungssätze', *Theoria*, iii (1937), pp. 330–42.

them. And if one decides to obey a command because one trusts the commanding person, or is afraid of disobeying, this has little to do with the theoretical evaluative foundations of that command. Finally, we should notice that the content of a command, being as a rule more practical, is *eo ipso* more concrete than the content of an 'analogous' value-judgement. Compare, for instance, 'it is good to get up early' with 'get up early'; *dulce et decorum est pro patria mori* and 'die for your country'.

Understanding value-judgements as a branch of imperatives or normative statements results in a rather disturbing picture of human relations. It presents the world as filled with the clamour of importunate despots and herdsmen, inhabited by individuals, who thirst to influence actively the behaviour of their neighbours, a world of commands and objections, obedience and rebellion. It does not seem to be a realistic picture. The majority of men appear to sense a difference between answers to the question 'how are we to evaluate action B' and the question 'what should I do in the situation where B is possible?' Kurt Baier also remarks that even the question 'what shall I do?' is very often asked 'not to be commanded, but to be advised. We ask for knowledge, deliberation, experience—not authority.'[1]

Two kinds of judgement are particularly troublesome for imperativists: assessment of past actions and aesthetic appraisals. When on the grounds of Heredotus' report we evaluate the behaviour of Cyrus and Cambyses, do our judgements really function as commands or prescriptions? We can deem Cyrus to have been a good ruler, although we certainly would not wish our rulers to behave like he did. Neither is our judgement simply a 'quotation' of opinion contemporary to Cyrus; in our assessment of the king of Persia we apply specific criteria, based on a historical perspective, and other than used to evaluate, say, eighteenth-century monarchs.

Let us suppose, however, that we accept Hare's theory and understand the judgement 'Cyrus was a good ruler' as analogous to, or containing, a moral command. (If a judgement does not contain an imperative, it is not, according to Hare, evaluative.) This command, addressed apparently to present and future rulers, would prescribe to them behaviour similar to the behaviour of

[1] K. Baier, *The Moral Point of View*, p. 56.

Cyrus. Whatever that similarity may consist in, the command makes sense only if, issuing it, we are able to imagine a present or future situation, in which a ruler could behave as Cyrus did. But such an interpretation of the judgement seems overstrained. If we define the similarity in terms sufficiently general to allow for analogies between, say, Haile Selassie and Cyrus, we shall see that our judgement has lost most of its rapport with facts, although a command, unrelated to facts, can hardly be considered a command. But it is, after all, quite possible to discuss in moral categories the actions of Cyrus and Cambyses, using the criteria of honesty and benevolence which we consider appropriate to their times and circumstances. Value-judgements, forming the conclusions of such discussions, would make 'no difference to what anybody has to do', although such practical implication is, according to Hare, a necessary condition of moral discourse.[1]

If one wishes to apply the imperativist conceptual framework in analysing aesthetic evaluation, a thorny problem springs up: what is commended or prescribed and to whom? When we read that Mozart was a great composer, or that *Et in Arcadia ego* is a beautiful picture, do we have to understand these judgements as prescriptions for composers and painters, or for listeners and viewers? The analogy with ethical judgements, which are to be interpreted as prescribing something to men who find themselves in situations similar to the person evaluated in the given judgement, would suggest the former possibility. It looks, however, so absurd ('compose like Mozart', 'paint like Poussin'), that we have to reject it forthwith. But the latter eventuality does not look too promising either: what is, in fact, commended? Aesthetic pleasure, or something else? What kind of pleasure to be attained by listening to *Cosi fan tutte*, or looking at Poussin's canvas, is commended, to whom, and why? And ought we to enjoy them in the same way as their contemporaries? These questions are left unanswered by the imperativist theory.

13.3 Let us now consider the other interpretation of the doctrine: that value-judgements imply, or even entail, normative statements. This requires at least a brief look at the problems of the logic of

---

[1] Hare, *Freedom and Reason*, p. 90.

imperatives, norms, and obligations. But first a terminological point.

Regrettably, statements of obligation ('ought' statements), and normative statements in general, are often called 'value-judgements'. This misleading custom plays, of course, into the hands of imperativists, but it also causes a lot of confusion, because the structure, function, and logic of these two types of utterances are by no means identical. There are many value-judgements which are evidently not normative ('Praxiteles was a great sculptor'), and normative statements which are not evaluative ('a child should sleep for at least 9 hours per day'). Whatever their similarities and mutual links, a common name covers them with a uniform and opaque blanket.

Furthermore, neither the imperativists nor their critics differentiate between imperatives ('do A'), statements of obligation ('X ought to do A'), and norms ('A ought to be done'). Imperativists assume that commanding is a necessary component of evaluation, and give examples of value-judgements and imperatives to illustrate their point. However, in presenting their thesis that value-judgements imply practical prescriptions they normally give examples simply in the form of normative statements. Many ambiguities and occasional muddles result. I shall not dwell on these, granting that the connection, whatever it may be, between evaluative and normative statements is an important axiological issue; but I do not think that the imperativists describe this connection in a fair manner.

Their main contention can be, somewhat crudely, summed up in the statement that 'A is good' entails 'you ought to do A'. This assertion seems, on the face of it, to contradict the celebrated rule—the origin of which is ascribed to Hume—that normative statements cannot be logically deduced from descriptive statements. The contradiction is only apparent, as imperativists make their thesis true by definition and do not consider 'A is good' an 'is' statement. Still, the 'is–ought' problem is so essential to modern ethics that, although it does not concern value-judgements in the strict sense, we have to give it some attention.

The fact of an obligation obtaining, or a norm being involved, is designated by verbs 'ought to' or 'should'. They may, however, be used in at least five different ways; so different as to give rise to distinct senses for these terms. They may refer:

(1) to the fact that the speaker expects something to happen: 'The bus ought to (should) come any minute now';

(2) to the fact that the given object or person is expected, or required, to possess certain features, without which it would be either substandard, or classified as belonging to some other class: 'A tire should have at least 2 mm. of tread', 'A guardsman ought to be at least six foot tall';

(3) to the fact of a demand which the speaker makes with respect to somebody: 'You ought to come here right away';

(4) to the fact that the subject of the sentence deserves something: 'He ought to be punished', 'He should be getting more money for what he does';

(5) to the fact of an obligation or a duty: 'Adam ought to pay John his debt', 'Soldiers should defend their country'.

This quintuple meaning of 'ought to' and 'should' is not a peculiarity of English; we observe it also, e.g., in German 'sollen', Polish 'powinien', or Russian 'dolzhen'. Unfortunately, different senses of 'ought' are rarely kept distinct. In everyday use the first and second are frequently mixed with the fourth and fifth; also, private expectations mingle with established, defining criteria and standards. The third sense tends to invade all others excepting the first. Even philosophers are apt to confuse 'ought' in the sense of a demand with 'ought' in the sense of obligation of duty; thus 'John ought to go to Manchester' in the sense that he is duty bound to do it is often taken as identical with 'John ought to go to Manchester' in the sense that we demand that he does it. The fourth and fifth sense are notoriously banded together, although the former refers to an obligation or duty owing *to*, and the latter to an obligation or duty *of* someone; thus the addressees, and possibly also supporting reasons, maybe even principles, are in each case different.

Sense three and sense five may, and frequently do, overlap: when Richard says to Peter 'You ought to help your mother immediately', he apparently not only demands from Peter that he help his mother, but also points to his duty to do so. But it is also possible to use 'ought' in statements which as a whole are opposed to somebody's fulfilling his obligation: 'Jack ought (is obliged) to pay his debt to Paul, but he ought not (we do not ask him) to do it, because Paul spends all his money on drugs.'

For axiology only meanings four and five are important and, when philosophers discuss the perplexing 'is–ought question', they ostensibly have only these senses in mind; as we shall see, however, other senses sometimes sneak in and obscure the issue.

It is sometimes assumed that 'ought' in the sense of obligation or duty is a thoroughly and typically ethical concept, but this is an oversimplification. Not only because not all duties and obligations belong to the sphere of morality ('before commencing the experiment, a bacteriologist ought to sterilize all his implements'), but also because the line between moral and non-moral duties and obligations, frequently difficult to draw, in real life is of little import. Empirically, most—although not all—obligations and duties are social facts, and their bonding force depends on the cohesiveness of the social fabric, which rarely ever allows for a clearcut classification of aspects.

13.4 There is some difference of opinion regarding what in fact Hume had in mind in his famous denial of the possibility of deriving 'ought' from 'is'.[1] Whatever he meant, the issue can be roughly presented as follows. Let f stand for a descriptive statement, or a set of descriptive statements, and o for an 'ought' statement. Is it possible to find an f and an o such that it would be self-contradictory to assert both f and not-o? If it is indeed possible to show that for some f and some o the formula $f \& \sim o$ is self-contradictory, then one succeeds in disproving Hume's contention.

Two recent attempts at such disproof have deservedly attracted much attention. Max Black gave the following example:

Fischer wants to mate Botwinnik.
The one and only way to mate Botwinnik is for Fischer to move the Queen.
Therefore, Fischer should move the Queen.[2]

---

[1] See papers by A. C. MacIntyre, R. F. Atkinson, G. Hunter, A. Flew, and W. D. Hudson in *The Is/Ought Question*, ed. W. D. Hudson, (London, 1969).

[2] M. Black, 'The Gap Between "Is" and "Should"', originally published in 1964 and reprinted in *The Is/Ought Question*, pp. 99–113.

This reasoning closely resembles the so-called practical syllogism: X wants A; he will not get A unless he does B; X has to do B.[1] But the cohesiveness of the practical syllogism, and also of Black's example, rests on a hidden tautology, because 'wants' can be developed into 'is resolved to do whatever is needed to achieve the object of his wish'. If Fischer does not make the move which he should make to mate Botwinnik, we shall say that he either did not see the possibility, or did not really want to mate Botwinnik. Fischer is under an obligation—to himself—to move the Queen because, and only because, he wants to mate Botwinnik; this is a case of a self-imposed norm. But this norm is present already in the concept 'wants', not only in 'ought'.[2]

Black's example offers a good opportunity to illustrate the variety of possible meanings of 'ought'. One may say:

To become the world champion Fischer ought to—it is a condition that he does—mate Botwinnik. (Second sense.)

Fischer ought—is obliged by his wish—to move the Queen. (Fifth sense.)

But he ought not to—we demand that he does not—do it, because for Botwinnik a lost match will be a personal tragedy. (Third sense.)

But Fischer is merciless, and ought—we expect him—to mate Botwinnik. (First sense.)

But he ought not—he does not deserve—to mate Botwinnik, because he is a vain man. (Fourth sense.)

Of course, the 'ought' following from 'is', or rather from 'wants', is the 'ought' of the second statement. Taking 'ought' in this—fifth—sense, we would consider it self-contradictory, if it were maintained that Fischer wants to mate Botwinnik, that to move the Queen is the only way to achieve this end, and that he ought not to move the Queen.

---

[1] According to G. H. von Wright, it is a logically valid formula, although it cannot be incorporated into 'ordinary logic'. Von Wright, *The Varieties of Goodness*, p. 167.

[2] Does such a self-imposed norm have as broad a scope as Kant thought when he wrote 'Who wills the end, wills also (necessarily, if he accords with reasons) the sole means which are in his power'? (*The Moral Law*, transl. H. J. Paton, London, 1947, p. 85.) Psychological observation does not seem to confirm this thesis.

Black's example does not destroy 'Hume's Guillotine', as he calls it, but curtails its functioning. It demonstrates that the verb 'to want', apparently purely 'descriptive', may be seen as containing a normative element similar to the one contained in the terms 'ought', 'should', and 'be obliged'. In other words, the fact of wanting something may, under certain circumstances, oblige the wanting person to obey specific rules of action; the same seems to apply to other terms, signifying intentions: 'desire', 'wish', 'strive for'. This obligation is, of course, undertaken by the subject himself and applies only to him.

John R. Searle presented a different example, based on the verb 'promise':

(1) Jones uttered the words 'I hereby promise to pay you, Smith, five dollars'.

(2) Jones promised to pay Smith five dollars.

(3) Jones placed himself under (undertook) an obligation to pay Smith five dollars.

(4) Jones is under an obligation to pay Smith five dollars.

(5) Jones ought to pay Smith five dollars.[1]

Again, as with 'wants', 'promised' can be interpreted as a term, committing its subject to do something. But there are also important differences. If Fischer deliberately does not move the Queen, we shall say that he did not want to mate Botwinnik and thus was not obliged to make the move. If Jones deliberately does not pay Smith five dollars, we may still say that he ought to do it; and if, having made his promise, he refuses to admit that he is under an obligation to pay, we may say that he made a false promise, not that he did not promise.

More importantly, it is, I think, at least highly debatable whether the passages from 'promise' to 'be under an obligation', and from 'be under an obligation' to 'ought', are really analytic. It is contradictory to say that an object A is red and that it is colourless; but it does not seem contradictory—at least, not in the same way, not so much, if you wish—to say that 'I promised but I am not under an obligation', 'I am under an obligation, but I should not', *unless* of course it is clearly understood that 'promise',

[1] 'How to Derive "Ought" from "Is"', *Is/Ought Question*, p. 127.

'obligation', and 'ought' or 'should' are here understood in the sense which Professor Searle calls 'institutional'—i.e., that 'ought' is here used in its *second* sense, as pointing to a condition which the given object has to satisfy to be classified as such. In this case, for a promiser to be classified as a non-substandard promiser, he has to be considered under an obligation and as one who ought to do what he has promised. But the transition from 'promised' to 'ought' in the fifth sense cannot be accomplished without several additional stipulations, which turn the whole reasoning into an artificial tautology.

Why are 'ought' statements, and statements of obligation, so fickle? Miss G. E. M. Anscombe provides part of the answer in her paper on 'Modern Moral Philosophy'. 'Ought'—in the fifth sense, of course—is genetically bound to a 'law conception of ethics'.[1] Amplifying her statement we may say that with the decline of belief in any generally binding moral laws, and in an all-embracing world order,[2] 'ought' has become a word of a 'mesmeric force', but loose on its hinges, Unless it is clearly specified which rule, or principle, or general norm, is supposed to apply in a given case, it is impossible to say whether anything ought to be done, or whether anybody is obliged to do anything. In the case of 'want' we have to do with a self-imposed norm, and this makes the situation comparatively simple; in the case of 'promise'—unless, I repeat, taken 'institutionally'—for any 'ought', several 'ought nots' can be produced. In other words, as there are many value systems, so there are corresponding to them many normative systems, sometimes mutually exclusive, frequently conflicting. A given value-language may encompass not only evaluative terms, but also normative terms, and rules for their usage.

13.5 But still, there surely is a point in what Searle says; a point

---

[1] *Is/Ought Question*, p. 176. Miss Anscombe is wrong in maintaining that belief in God is necessary for law-ethics: the ethics of honour also belong to this type, although it does not assume the existence of God as the law-giver. But she is right in saying that the most important systems of law-ethics have been based on religious beliefs. They have mostly contributed to the latent meaning of 'ought'.

[2] Where such beliefs persist, as in many ideologically rigid groups, 'ought' is taken to follow from statements of fact.

analogous to the one made by Black. To clarify this point we have to place the whole problem in the broader context of semiotics.

First, it has to be noted that it is not the *act* of uttering the words 'I promise', or 'I want', which commits one, or makes us consider the person uttering them under an obligation, to behave in a certain way: it is the *meaning* attached to these words and to the whole statement of which they form a part. An act by itself does not commit anybody to do anything, unless in the crudely physical sense of determining his next possible moves. Furthermore, acts cannot be consistent with each other, but only with some principles of action. The *fact* of saying 'the sky is blue' does not commit one to denying any proposition which contradicts this statement. It is only accepting this statement as true which imposes specific norms concerning the acceptance of other propositions. If a statement is self-contradictory, or patently absurd, it is difficult to imagine (let alone systematize) the consequences of its acceptance. Similarly, if one utters the words: 'I promise to live three hundred years', or 'I promise to make gold out of copper', we would hardly consider this person obliged to do what he has promised.

Although they deal ostensibly with the 'is–ought' question, both Black and Searle use terms which themselves present serious difficulties if one tries to render them by straightforward 'is' formulae. Both 'want' and 'promise' belong to a semantic category which I shall call 'committal terms': they cannot be unqualifiedly predicated of a person without his being understood to be committed to a specific kind of future behaviour.[1] They are not the only members of this class: 'accept'[2] and 'believe' are much more important. It was presumably their insistence on calling 'ought' an evaluative rather than a normative term which has prevented moral philosophers from noticing that the 'is–ought' question may be taken as part of a much broader, not necessarily ethical, issue.

---

[1] 'Consistency' and 'commitment' may, broadly speaking, mean either of the two: 1. a relation between principles and behaviour; this does not, as a rule, concern us here; and 2. a relation between statements. In natural language this second type of consistency and commitment is always a matter of approximation.

[2] In any science, the adopted acceptability rules commit the scientist to accept certain propositions or data.

Let us have a look at the following group of statements—patently descriptive, and thus either true or false:

(1) A believes that p.
(2) A accepts p as true.
(3) A wants s.
(4) A wishes that s.
(5) A promises s.
(6) A renounces s.

Each of these, if accepted as true, imposes certain commitments, e.g.:

(1) If A believes that p, and knows that $p \rightarrow q$, A should also believe that q.[1]

(2) If A accepts that p, A ought not to accept that $\sim p$.

(3) If A wants s, and $u \rightarrow \sim s$, A ought not to want u.

(4) If A wishes that s, and s comes to pass, A ought not to be sorry.[2]

(5) If A promises s, and w is the only and sufficient means to secure s, A should do w.

(6) If A renounces s, and s is given to him, A should not appear overjoyed.

Of course—this has to be stressed again—our everyday language being what it is, these commitments are not absolutely binding. In our examples, the force of committal, implied by the predicate, seems to decrease from the strongest in 'believe' to the weakest in 'renounce'. More importantly, there may be various degrees of acceptance,[3] belief, wanting, and wishing; a renunciation or a promise may be taken more or less seriously by both givers and takers. What follows is not only that commitment, or implication, may vary in their content and strength, but seemingly also that propositions with predicates like 'accept', 'believe', and 'want' can be true or false in various degrees. The only way to avoid this

---

[1] See J. Hintikka, *Knowledge and Belief* (Ithaca, N.Y., 1962), pp. 23-9 and *passim*; N. Rescher, *Topics in Philosophical Logic* (Dordrecht, 1968), pp. 40-53.

[2] Similar consistency, but still looser and more difficult to pin down, is expected in the case of emotional states and attitudes, such as love, hate, envy.

[3] R. M. Martin, *Toward a Systematic Pragmatics* (Amsterdam, 1959), p. 12.

rather awkward conclusion is to state that for any given 'strength' of 'accept', 'believe', etc., there are corresponding commitments and consequences, which either are fulfilled, making the proposition true, or unfulfilled, in which case it is false.

If these remarks do not seem to hold for 'promise' and 'renounce', this is because both these terms have their 'institutional' connotations, which stiffen their meaning although they do not always determine their actual function. But the difference is only superficial. A promising person has to decide within which system of values and norms he will place his promise. This decision is equivalent to determining the degree of acceptance. We may never know what the decision was; therefore, as said above, the implication of obligation in 'promise' and 'renounce' is the weakest. Outside an institutional framework, these terms may be considered from the point of view of so many divergent normative systems, that their binding force is frequently a matter of guesswork.

Do the committal terms really represent an exception to the rule that normative statements do not logically follow from descriptive statements? I do not think so. They qualify the rule in an important way, but do not destroy it. The transition from 'is' to 'ought' requires not only logic, but also psychology. One has to *decide* to accept a proposition as true, or to believe something, or to want something, or to promise; and then one must show enough determination to accept the commitment which such a decision implies. Thus, if not an act of will—by which one may simply adopt an 'ought to' rule—then some other, analogous, psychological act or attitude is necessary to bridge the gap between 'is' and 'ought'.

13.6 Imperativists do not reject Hume's Guillotine; on the contrary, they invoke it in their own favour. Their contention that value-judgements entail normative statements rests on their conception of value-judgements as utterances, the characteristic feature of which is, indeed, a normative implication. According to Hare, the 'first principles', which direct our evaluative reasoning, 'must contain implicitly or explicitly an imperative'.[1] These

---

[1] A. MacIntyre says that Hare was 'a pioneer in the logical investigation of imperatives' (*Short History of Ethics*, p. 261). But Hare's logic of imperatives has its predecessor in H. Poincaré: 'Si les prémisses d'un syllogisme sont toutes les deux à l'indicatif, la conclusion sera également à l'indicatif. Pour que la

principles have usually the form of value-judgements; the imperative is contained in the evaluative predicate. 'Good' and kindred
predicates entail 'ought'—this is the fundamental axiological
thesis of imperativism. It is supposed to apply primarily, or exclusively, to moral contexts.

Leaving aside for the moment the risky idea of seaparating the
sphere of morality from everything else, we must ask whether our
judgement that someone is good always implies an obligation?
And if so, what is the scope of that obligation? 'St. Francis was a
good man'—ought all men, or only some (why? how selected?) to
behave like the monk of Assisi? A man who devotes his life to
bringing up orphans does good; and so does a man who lives alone
and makes important scientific discoveries. We do not see any discrepancy between these evaluative judgements, although they
would entail divergent obligations. But the theory of such entailment has dubious foundations and is of questionable usefulness,
both philosophically and practically. This is even more evident in
the case of evaluative predicates, the meaning of which is bound
with concrete ideals: 'heroic', 'humble', 'complaisaint', 'steadfast'.
We may evaluate positively, and even admire, men displaying these
qualities, without at the same time recommending analogous
behaviour. Imperativism seems to imply a practical monism of
moral ideals.

The theory of entailed imperatives or obligations has yet another
hidden weakness. We expect from norms, statements of obligation,
and commands that they be fairly concrete, as they have an immediate practical function. But the entailment theory does not
allow for such a concreteness of content, as it does not even state

conclusion peût être mise à l'imperatif, il faudrait que l'une des premises au
moins fût elle-même à l'imperatif.' (*Dernières Pensées*, Paris, 1913, p. 225.)
And Hare's main thesis, 'No imperative conclusion can be validly drawn from
a set of premises which does not contain at least one imperative' (*Language of
Morals*, p. 28) not only echoes Poincaré, but repeats Dubislav's statement:
'Dabei zeigt sich, dass man keinen Forderungssatz aus Foraussetzungen sensu
stricto ableiten kann, die nich selber mindestens einen Forderungssatz
enthalten.' (See note 3, p. 99, above.) See also Alf Ross, 'Imperatives and
Logic', *Philosophy of Science* (1944), pp. 30–46, and N. Rescher, *The Logic of
Commands* (London, 1966), pp. 73–4.

which sense of 'ought' is entailed. And what is the framework of the allegedly implied obligations? Is it the framework indicated by the descriptive reference of evaluative predicates, i.e., if somebody is said to be generous, is the content of the entailed obligation determined by what are the commonly understood empirical features of acts of generosity? This would be to take 'ought' in its second, 'institutional' sense. But such an interpretation seems to run counter to the essence of imperativism and, besides, would lead not to accepting the entailment doctrine, only to investigating the coherence of socially functioning value systems. And, after all, it is a well-known truth that it is easier to evaluate some quality as good than to say how to achieve this quality; thus, imperativism demands too much from value-judgements, and promises us more than we can get from them.

Value-judgements are statements, the analysis of which poses many irritating difficulties, but the theory of entailment, supposed to elucidate the essence of these judgments, explains *obscurum* by *obscurius*.

13.7 What is the relation of value-judgements, taken within the theoretical pattern of evaluation, to statements of obligation, norms, and imperatives? It is impossible to deduce a normative statement, let alone an imperative, from a value-judgement or a value-principle. Although the statement 'X is good, therefore you ought —or, it is obligatory—to do X' sounds reasonable, this is not the reasonableness of an inference, but of a supporting argument, the acceptance or rejection of which is a matter of decision. On a similar decision hinges the acceptance or rejection of the argument 'you should—therefore do!'.

I am unable to discuss here at any length the complex question of kinds of argumentation which may connect value-judgements, normative statements, and imperatives. Let us only note that, as when we use the practical syllogism (see 13.4) to connect descriptive with normative statements, in connecting value-judgements with 'ought' statements we also have to rely on the meaning of 'to want', or a similar term, and not on the meaning of evaluative predicates. Thus the value-principle 'honesty is a good' can be linked to the norm 'one ought to be honest' by means of the conditional clause 'if one wants': 'if one wants to be good, one ought to be honest'. The value-judgement 'John is trustworthy' can be connected with the normative statement 'you ought to behave like John does' by means of the clause 'if you want to be trustworthy', or with the norm 'you ought to be trustworthy' by means of the clause 'if you want to be like John'. The same, *mutadis mutandis*, applies to Kant's so-called hypothetical imperative: 'killing is evil'—'if you do not want to do evil, do not kill'.

Without investigating any further problem of possible relations and dependence, we can note the generally accepted *direction* of the argument. It goes, in ascending order, from imperatives through normative statements to evaluative judgements and value-principles. The imperative 'do not steal' is supported by the norm 'one ought not to steal'. This norm is, in turn, supported by the principle 'stealing is wrong'. It would be nonsensical to reverse the order: 'stealing is wrong, because you ought not to steal', or, 'you would do wrong not telling the truth, because do not lie'. The only exceptions to this 'rule of direction' are arguments like: 'Adam did wrong when he panicked, because one ought not to panic.' This exception is explainable by the fact that general norms play sometimes the role of substitutes of value-principles. We should not, however, say 'killing is wrong because one ought not to kill', but vice versa, 'one ought not to kill, because killing is wrong'.

Thus, whatever the above kinds of argumentation are worth, their natural direction runs counter to Hare's tenet concerning the imperatives contained already in the first principles of evaluative reasoning. Hare is evidently impressed by the motivational force of these first principles. But what is most momentous is not that his thesis reverses the natural direction of thought, but that it obscures the differences between its components, lumping imperatives, value-principles, norms, statements of obligation, and value-judgements into one almost homogeneous whole. If we accepted Hare's conception, we should become obliged to regard this multiplicity of forms as superfluous and apply to it some form of Ockham's razor. But value-judgements, normative statements, and imperatives differ from each other both in their meaning and in their function, and are at least partly independent.

13.8 Hare's insistence on the imperative essence of all evaluative and normative statements may be explained by the fact that in this way he seeks to demonstrate the existence of universally binding moral norms. To this purpose, he formulates the 'universalizability thesis', which says that 'the meaning of the word "ought" and other moral words is such that a person who uses them commits himself thereby to a universal rule'.[1] In other words, when somebody utters a moral judgement, or a normative statement, concerning a certain act, he *eo ipso* commits himself to pass the same judgement on all acts similar 'in the relevant respects'.[2]

The universalizability thesis provokes three objections. First, the decision as to which respects are relevant would in most cases be based on an evaluation. Hare proposes as the criterion of the relevance of a given characteristic the fact that one considers it relevant irrespective of whether it is oneself or somebody else who displays it.[3] However, this proposal boils down to a postulate of fairness and has not much to do with the logic of argument. If somebody refuses to be fair in his judgements or, more likely, maintains that he has sufficient reasons to treat others differently from the way he treats himself—we may detest the man but still find it hard to point at a fault in his logic. The fairness principle may be a respectable criterion for evaluating moral attitudes and values, but it is of little use in describing the structure and content of moral reasoning.[4] We usually do not, and hardly ever can, know whether a given judgement was expressed by a person who was ready to conform to the universalizability rule. But this has nothing to do with the soundness of the judgement itself. A thoroughly corrupt person—like Talleyrand—may offer incisive judgments of others. Shall we disqualify these judgements because their author does not seem to subscribe to the universalizability thesis? It would be highly impractical to make the sense of a judgement dependent on the presumed attitude of its utterer. In short, the coherence of fairness postulated by the universalizability

---

[1] Hare, *Freedom and Reason*, p. 30.
[2] Ibid., p. 11.   [3] Ibid., pp. 102–7.
[4] Hare explicitly requires that, for a judgement to be 'moral', it has to be understood as conforming to the universalizability thesis (e.g., *Language of Morals*, p. 100). But in doing this he prescribes a particular moral doctrine, arbitrarily delimiting the scope of morality.

thesis is a moral and psychological, not a logical principle, and is therefore evaluative not analytic.

Secondly, the universalizability thesis assumes tacitly the equality of men, and openly a convergence of their interests.[1] If we do not assume that the rights, duties, and needs of all men are either the same, or at least commensurably isomorphic, any attempt to apply the universalizability rule will entangle us in the vicious circle of evaluation. Hare maintains that the universalizability thesis makes it possible for ethics to be 'relevant to moral decisions without ceasing to be neutral'.[2] But this is not quite true. For instance, in medieval ethics the duties of a knight were different from the duties of his page, not to mention a peasant; the difference of status would not allow for universalization. Neither the morality of a full realization of one's potential, so characteristic of the Renaissance, nor nineteenth-century evolutionist ethics can be reconciled with the universalizability thesis—nor even described as 'moral' if one adopts Hare's standpoint. A hero, offering his life for others, may do so on the strength of a belief that, as stronger and braver than his companions, he makes it unnecessary for them to do what he does. There are objects and men of whom it is better that they remain unique; not because they are not 'wholly good' and praiseworthy, but because their value resides, at least partly, in their very uniqueness, and is not reproducible or repeatable. When we morally evaluate Buddha, Jesus Christ, or Gandhi, do we understand our evaluation in the way required by the universalizability thesis? Revolutionary movements too are an example of a mass rejection of the universalizability thesis, a rejection undertaken, paradoxically, in the name of the postulate of equality implied by that thesis—which, as the whole doctrine to which it belongs, ignores history.

---

[1] See *Freedom and Reason*, p. 177: 'it is characteristic of moral thought in general to accord equal weight to the interests of all persons.' This sentence can be understood either as a definition of morality—narrow and totally ahistorical—or as an empirical statement—evidently false. It is true that modern moralists (but not all, see Nietzsche) usually assume that men are 'more or less equal' (see Sir Isaiah Berlin, 'Equality', *Proceedings of the Aristotelian Society*, 1955–6, pp. 304–5). But if we do not consider the principle of equality a tautology, then it is either a postulate, or an evaluative principle—and certainly not an empirical finding.   [2] Hare, *Freedom and Reason*, p. 88; see also p. 97.

Thirdly, the universalizability principle, which resembles both the ancient Golden Rule ('treat others as you wish them to treat you') and Kant's categorical imperative, shares with them a common weakness. Namely, it is possible, in full accord with this purely formal rule, to proclaim and impose any principles to whose application to oneself one consents. Any advocate of a 'chosen' people or group ideology may underwrite this principle and proceed to persecute, in the name of some 'logic of history', anyone who disobeys his rules of world order.

Thus, the universalizability principle is neither ethically neutral, nor does it provide us with grounds to develop a fuller moral programme. It smuggles in certain specific ethical assumptions, but leaves the rest to intuition and individual decision. And imperativism does not provide tools to prepare such a decision discursively and to discuss its content.[1]

13.9 The emotivists' concept of 'emotive meaning' has its counterpart in the imperativists' notions of 'prescriptive', 'commendatory', or 'imperative' meaning. A majority of the objections raised above against the concept of 'emotive meaning' can also be applied to the latter group. It is possible to conclude from Hare's own statements that the presence of prescriptive meaning is always a matter of guesswork. He admits that in many cases we use evaluative predicates without this kind of meaning.[2] The supposition that prescriptive meaning is peculiar to evaluation is undermined by the simple observation that some obviously declarative-descriptive statements, like 'this snake is poisonous', 'there's cheap meat at the butcher's today', 'the mushrooms on your plate are inedible', perform a much more prominently imperative functions than, e.g., 'John is an honest fellow'. Hare's doctrine of typically prescriptive meaning of all evaluative predicates is simply a consequence of putting normative and evaluative statements into one pen, and thus is a result not of observation, but of a terminological decision.

Philosophically more momentous is his thesis that, although evaluative terms are not devoid of descriptive meaning, it is always secondary to the evaluative, i.e., prescriptive, meaning.[3] This is

---

[1] See A. MacIntyre, *A Short History of Ethics*, pp. 261–2.
[2] Hare, *Language of Morals*, pp. 124–5; *Freedom and Reason*, pp. 68, 190.
[3] Hare, *Language of Morals*, p. 148.

supposed to apply particularly to 'good'. The 'secondariness thesis' may be interpreted in two ways, as applying either to (1) the genesis of prescriptive meaning, or to (2) its frequency and prominence.

(1) The etymology of 'good' unequivocally contradicts the idea of the primacy of its prescriptiveness. Greek '*agathos*' traces its source to 'free born', 'of noble origin'. English 'good' has its origins in a word meaning 'fit', 'appropriate'. Polish '*dobry*' has a common root with '*godny*', 'deserving'.[1] It may be asserted without any doubt that the genesis of the concept 'good' is not in some encouraging exclamation or command, but in words signifying certain objects or qualities which for concrete reasons came to be considered valuable.

(2) If the basic meaning of 'good' was commendatory or prescriptive, the term would loosen its links with value systems and their criteria, and become primarily a means of propagating preferences. To support his thesis, Hare gives the following example:

Let us suppose that a missionary, armed with a grammar book, lands on a cannibal island. The vocabulary of his grammar book gives him the equivalent, in the cannibals' language, of the English word 'good'. Let us suppose that, by a queer coincidence, the word is 'good'. And let us suppose, also, that it really is the equivalent—that it is, as the *Oxford English Dictionary* put is, 'the most general adjective of commendation' in their language. If the missionary has mastered his vocabulary, he can, *so long as he uses the word evaluatively and not descriptively*, communicate with them about morals quite happily. They know that when he uses the word he is commending the person or object that he applies it to. The only thing they will find odd is that he applies it to such unexpected people, people who are meek and gentle and do not collect large quantities of scalps; whereas they themselves are accustomed to commend people who are bold and burly and collect more scalps than the average.[2]

His argumentation here contains a *petitio principii*: if we define

<hr/>

[1] H. G. Liddell and R. S. Scott, *A Greek-English Lexicon* (Oxford, 1925); W. W. Skeat, *An Etymological Dictionary of the English Language* (Oxford, 1879); F. Sławski, *Słownik etymologiczny języka polskiego*, (Cracow, 1956).

[2] Hare, *Language of Morals*, p. 148. The supposition that in a primitive society 'good' could be used for commendation severed from description, is, of course, contrary to all we know from cultural anthropology.

'good' as 'the most general adjective of commendation', there is no need to prove, and no possibility of proving, that it serves primarily for commendation and that its descriptive meaning is secondary to the evaluative-commendative, what the example affects to demonstrate.[1] But let us take the issue as an open one. If the cannibals really understand 'good' in the mouth of the missionary as pure commendation, the saintly chap can spare his breath and effort, and simply grin at the meek and gnash his teeth at the burly with their scalp collections: his commendations would then be expressed with equal clarity but more economically. Would we, however, call his grimaces 'communicating about morals'? Moral judgements are usually understood as something else and more than expressions of personal applause or disgust, and this is what the cannibals in Hare's tale are treated to.

13.10 One of the fundamental tenets of imperativism is that it is possible to sequester the sphere of moral discourse; this belief is a necessary component of the whole imperativist theory. For it is obvious that it would be absurd to ascribe an imperative meaning, or function, to predicates and statements in many non-ethical contexts. 'It is good to be a sportsman', 'it is good to know ten languages', 'it is good to discern the vintages of Nuits St. Georges' —we may readily agree with these evaluations but would consider nonsensical attempts at inferring from them any general or particular norms.

We have already discussed (§11) the impossibility of separating the ethical from other kinds of evaluation; let me add a few more words about this question. When men are considering a moral problem, they usually take into account many data and factors from outside the sphere of morality, without much bothering about their classification. To establish once and for all, and for all value systems, where the consequences of these extra-moral elements end, and where the 'autonomous' region of moral considerations begins—if it exists at all, is certainly impossible.

[1] This example is typical of Hare's method: he defines his basic concepts in such a way that finding examples which could contradict his theory is *a priori* excluded. This incontroversibility of his theory results in tautology and bars attempts at a verification. See also M. Warnock, *Ethics since 1900* (London, 1960), pp. 127-9.

Let us suppose that we have at our disposal a certain sum of money, and an amount of food, to be used for helping under-developed countries. Let us assume that we have to choose between two applicants, a primitive tribe, which is dying out from hunger and illness, and which in all probability will use up our help in a dissolute manner, raise its birth rate and promptly return to the present state of exhaustion, and a nation, which has at its disposal resources just sufficient to allow it to subsist on a low level of civilization, and to which our help may open up a distinct possibility of cultural development and economic prosperity. No-one will call this example artificial; it is certain that moral decisions are involved, but to separate them from considerations economic, social, cultural, and so on, is hardly possible. The problem of evaluating different models of societies undoubtedly has ethical aspects, but it is difficult to discuss it in 'purely ethical' terms.

13.11 While emotivism presents an excessively pessimistic picture of the possibilities of evaluative reasoning, Hare's imperativist theories of entailed prescriptions and of universalizability impute to value-judgements more logical stringency than observation and semantic analysis bear out.

The imperativist theory of evaluation obscures the difference in meaning and function between various types of expressions, linked to evaluation, and particularly between evaluative judgements on the one hand and normative statements on the other.

The purpose of the above critical comments has been not only to expose the weaknesses and ambiguities of imperativism, but also to prepare the ground for the thesis that, from a methodological point of view, it is more advantageous to treat value-principles and judgements as basic, and normative statements and imperatives as in some way dependent on them. This is the approach represented in ethics by, e.g., Brentano (*Wertethik*) and Moore, and in the general philosophy of value by Von Wright. Not the least important advantage of this standpoint is that it also makes it possible to consider on a broad plane of axiology aesthetic and other kinds of evaluation. The alternative position, pronouncing the primacy of norms over value-judgements—Kant's *Pflichtethik*—can be applied to ethics only, and results in isolating morality from other spheres of value.

§14. *The cognitive content of value-judgements*

14.1 It has been said above (§5.6) that the problem of the truth-value of evaluative judgements ought to be investigated from the point of view of the existence of many value-languages, bound to different value-systems. The question whether value-judgements can be true or false is equivalent to the question whether they can possess a cognitive content. Since the dominant opinions of our century have refused a truth-value to value-judgements, it is perhaps appropriate to return once more to this problem.

By and large, two objections have been raised against value-judgements' being true or false: (1) evaluative judgements express emotions, commands, or prescriptions, and either do not contain a cognitive content, or contain it only incidentally; (2) their content is so vague that it is uncertain which criteria of truth and falsity should be applied to them. The first objection has been discussed above in §§12 and 13; now I shall try briefly to answer the second.

If one accepts this argument, one is also compelled to refuse truth-value to all statements with predicates, the meaning of which varies with time, place, and environment: 'narrow', 'broad', 'high', 'poor', 'fast', and the like. For a tree 'high' in Lapland will be 'low' in Nigeria; a street 'broad, in the City of London will be 'narrow' in Houston, and the contemporary 'short' skirt would not have been a skirt at all some fifty years ago. (We may observe here that even 'skirt' may have an evaluative tinge, e.g., in the mouth of an elderly lady who says 'decent girls wear skirts and not these loin-cloths'.) Of course, these are extreme examples, but we may say generally that the truth or falsity of every statement, with predicates whose meaning is bound-up with historical, social, or cultural conventions, can be ascertained only by reference to the given context of that statement. The difference between statements asserting that somebody is noble, forbearing, and compassionate, and statements asserting that he is tall, slender, and dexterous, is not as great as is sometimes maintained.

Interpretative perplexities stem usually from the fact that 'vague' predicates are used within different value-languages. Within a specific value-language a term may have a pretty clear and well-defined meaning. The difficulty, then, is practical and consists not in some inherent elusiveness, but in the need for an initial clue to determine the interpretative framework.[1]

It is worth noting that evaluative predicates, as used in everyday parlance, appear less vague than it would seem from what philosophers tell us. In communicating about moral or aesthetic matters we can usually understand or find out fairly easily what the other person means—of course, within the limits of clarity and precision, appropriate to ordinary discourse. Equivocations of propagandists are quite simply pinned down by anyone with a keen mind. Serious difficulties begin when a philosophical analyst takes a judgement out of its situational context and begins to dissect it with a preciseness inappropriate to the rules and purposes of everyday speech. When we go shopping for groceries, we do not expect them to be weighed to the exact milligramme. Some philosophers wish that value predicates were precise like scientific terms; they would not expect the same from 'bright', 'soft', or 'spacious'.

14.2 The problem of the vagueness of value-judgements has to be distinguished from the problem of the generality of some evaluative predicates. 'Good', 'bad', 'valuable', 'valueless' usually have a general sense; it does not follow, however, that their meaning must be vague. (Nor should the fact that these predicates may take several meanings be confused with the problem of their vagueness or clarity.) R. M. Hare contends that 'good' is a 'loose word', and illustrates his thesis by the similarly 'loose' word 'hot': 'We can give quite simple and adequate criteria for deciding whether object X is hotter than object Y; but if we are asked to give exact criteria for saying whether an object is hot, we shall be quite unable to do so.'[2] But 'hot', like hundreds of other terms, appears so hopelessly 'loose' only when taken out of context, and if we try to attach to it

---

[1] M. Przełęcki proposes to settle the question of the logical value of propositions containing vague terms by interpreting a vague term as one denoting not a set of objects, but a certain family of sets. 'Each of these sets corresponds to a certain possible classification of objects from within the scope of vagueness of the predicate P, into those which fall under the predicate and those which do not.' M. Przełęcki, 'Filozoficzne konsekwencje semantycznej teorii prawdy', *Studia Filozoficzne* (1973), No. 6, p. 203.

[2] Hare, *Language of Morals*, p. 183.

fixed criteria of application. 'A hot summer day' in England would not be thought of as 'hot' in Italy; and if a gardener and a steel-mill worker disagree about the 'hotness' of something, it is not because they use 'hot' loosely, but because they apply different criteria.

'Good' may vie with 'idea' as the most written-about word in the history of philosophy. Is it really 'undefinable', as G. E. Moore asserted? Moore's concept of definition was so eccentric, and his arguments against the 'definist fallacy' (Frankena's term) so sweeping,[1] that he raised more questions than he set out to solve. And the ensuing debate, although it generated several important contributions,[2] frequently made the original confusion more confounding. Scanning the field of discussion produces several reflections:

(a) Moore's concept of definition was such as to preclude the possibility of *any* definition of 'good', and, in fact, of any definition which does not have the form of a list of properties. 'Visible', on his terms, is as indefinable as 'good'.

(b) His objections against the 'naturalist fallacy' are such as to apply also to non-naturalistic definitions of 'good': emotivist or imperativist.

(c) The controversy between 'naturalism' and 'non-naturalism' is an ethical, not a meta-ethical conflict. The claim that the ethical predicates can be clearly distinguished from the non-ethical ones forms a part of an ethical doctrine; and so does the opposite opinion. Whether ethical judgements can be adequately translated into statements about psychological or social facts depends on the kind of ethical values involved; whether they reflect some peculiar moral emotions or intuitions depends on the axiological framework applied. Whichever position is closer to the truth cannot be decided by means of a logical analysis of evaluation, because a moral doctrine may have its basic terms defined arbitrarily and, as long as it conforms to a coherent usage, an axiologist cannot say that they are used 'improperly'. From a meta-ethical point of view one can only investigate which of the competing ethical theories covers more

---

[1] See also M. Warnock, *Ethics since 1900*, pp. 16 ff.

[2] e.g., W. M. Frankena, 'The Naturalistic Fallacy' (1939), and P. T. Geach, 'Good and Evil' (1956), both reprinted in Philippa Foot, ed., *Theories of Ethics* (Oxford, 1967).

ground, which accounts for more phenomena. Otherwise, for an axiologist the naturalism–non-naturalism debate is like a debate about whether the British English or the American English is more correct.

(d) We may observe, however, that most naturalists and their adversaries persist in wallowing in Moore's original sin: naturalists look for one common denominator in all moral uses of 'good', for one *kind* of denotation of the term, while their emotivist and pre-scriptivist opponents also ascribe to 'good' a uniform psychological function.

(e) It is frequently maintained that 'good' implies preference—but, in fact, often it does not. Suppose that a second-hand car dealer asks me: 'Do you want a good car?' Knowing the implied criteria and the state of my purse, I answer: 'No, I want a fairly cheap and dependable old runner.' To a friend who says, 'I hope you are going to have good weather,' I may reply, 'I do not wish to have good weather; it is easier to work when it's cold and raining.'[1] Whenever there are stable and mutually comprehensible criteria of goodness, we may use the term and communicate happily without showing any preference for the 'good' object.

(f) What is, however, always implied in 'good', 'bad', etc., is the possibility of comparison with other similar objects. Whenever we call something 'good', we implicitly form a class of objects comparable in a certain respect, and select within this class an object which meets the assumed standards of comparison. What is the extension of that class and what are the standards we do not learn from 'good' alone and have to find out from its context, verbal and situational. But in this 'good' is not much different from 'hot', 'high', or 'fast'; knowing English, we know the meaning—more precisely, the connotation—of these words, but we have to identify in each case the criteria for their application. This does not mean, of course, that these criteria are arbitrarily established. Similarly

---

[1] These examples epitomize the evidence that 'good' is commonly used as referring not to personal preferences, but to mutually understood standards. More examples in Nowell-Smith, *Ethics*, pp. 170–1. It is arbitrary to call these uses of 'good' 'inverted commas' or 'conventional' uses; Hare's position on this point (*Language of Morals*, pp. 124–6) is typical of the radical individualism of his theory.

with 'good': we learn that an object of which it is predicated meets some implied standards and that, within the implied real or imaginary class of comparable objects, it occupies a special position. It is the position of a 'fully qualified' member; and we should not try to be too specific here, remembering the multiplicity of functions of 'good' and the impreciseness of natural languages. It has to suffice that the objects, about which 'good', 'bad', etc., are predicated, occupy extreme positions within the implied class of evaluated objects.

R. M. Hare, who also makes the distinction between the meaning and the criteria of 'good',[1] for some reason talks of meaning only in the sense of denotation and/or expressive function. However, the extension of the class of 'good' objects is in each case determined by the criteria, and, if in the meaning of 'good' anything remains stable, it is its connotation, which I have tried to characterize above.[2]

14.3 The way in which 'good' and other more general evaluative predicates function is best revealed by comparing them with other evaluative predicates—for instance, 'assiduous', 'severe', 'obedient'. A 'good man' is one who meets some basic standards of judgement, imposed by the given value-system; an 'assiduous man' is one whose behaviour displays the quality of assiduousness, probably, but it is not clear to what degree, positively evaluated. A 'good teacher' is one who does meet some basic requirements set for teachers within the given value-system; a 'severe teacher' is one whose behaviour possesses the quality of severity, which may be negatively or positively evaluated. Similarly, 'good soldier' and 'obedient soldier'.

Compared to other evaluative predicates, general predicates display greater evaluative precision and a greater descriptive vague-

[1] Hare, *Language of Morals*, pp. 96–110.
[2] See K. Aschenbrenner, *The Concepts of Value : Foundations of Value Theory* (Dordrecht, 1971), p. 371: 'The good, or *good*, as we see it, is an ultimate and somewhat abstract notion. It is ultimate in the sense that it may presuppose for its clarification or support any and all of the whole previous train of appraisive concepts. It is without significance except in reference to them, and so far as evidence is concerned they are all independent of it. Its generality rests on the fact that it is the only notion that may be involved in *all* of the foregoing'.

ness. The judgement 'John is a good man' does not leave any doubt as to the fact that it expresses a positive appraisal; it may be uncertain, however, what the criteria are on which the judgement has been made. The judgement 'John is a persistent man' informs unambiguously about certain features of John's behaviour, but it may leave open the question whether his persistence is just reported, or also evaluated—positively, or negatively.

To explain the reason why the meaning of general evaluative predicates differs in kind from the meaning of other evaluative predicates[1] is to indicate what is their peculiar function. Now, uncertainty either as to the criteria on which the given use of a general evaluative predicate is based, or as to the evaluative sense of ordinary evaluative predicates, results from the fact that we do not always know within which value-language the given judgement ought to be placed. But any misunderstanding in evaluative matters may be seriously harmful to our relations with other people. Hence the need, especially urgent in the case of comparative judgements, to use the general evaluative predicates, which make our evaluations unambiguous, although their links with the actual criteria used are sometimes elusive. In other words, the general evaluative predicates form a bridge between particular value-languages and the national language. The specificity of their function is rarely ever fully acknowledged by axiologists (Aschenbrenner is the most notable exception), and this obfuscates the differences between value predicates of various degrees of generality and leads to many other misunderstandings. It is mistaken, for instance, to maintain on the basis of an analysis of 'good' that all, or most, evaluative predicates have an equally elusive rapport with concrete criteria.

14.4 The question of the possible verification of value-judgements is often confused with the issue of accepting given value-principles. When, for instance, Carnap writes that the statement '"Killing is evil" . . . is neither true nor false. It does not assert anything and can neither be proved nor disproved',[2] he is in a sense quite right,

---

[1] The distinction is not sharp, but gradual; see 'excellent', 'noble', 'fine', 'beautiful', and so on.

[2] R. Carnap, *Philosophy and Logical Syntax*, p. 24.

because the judgement cited is a typical value-principle, accepted or rejected in a way analogous to the acceptance or rejection of axioms or basic premisses (see §16). But Carnap's thesis is generally understood as applying to ordinary evaluative judgements. Thus interpreted, it rests on an absolutist concept of truth and on a traditional, absolutist and idealist, concept of value. An absolutist concept of truth lacks any reference to the given language, on the basis of which a given sentence is actually interpreted; an absolutist concept of value holds that there exists only one set of exclusive and universally true value-judgements. It is clear that an empiricist like Carnap has to reject the possibility of granting logical value to these 'absolutely true' judgements, as they can not be verified or falsified by reference to facts and rules of logic. But absolutist concepts of value are not the only ones possible. Carnap and other philosophers, refusing to value-judgements any possibility of verification, set for them anachronistic requirements, transplanted whole from philosophical systems having little to do with logical empiricism. This is a case analogous to the application, by Ayer, of a rigid concept of description (see §5.2).

If we assume that value-judgements can be true or false within the terms of given value-languages, their verification, although practically complex, appears theoretically feasible. For instance, statements that it is right to sterilize incurables, or to apply euthanasia, are false in the context of Roman Catholic ethics; and a statement that it is better to break your word than to risk death is false in the context of the ethics of honour.

When is a value-judgement false? (1) When the facts, mentioned in the judgement, are wrong; e.g., 'Napoleon displayed great courage in the battle of Crécy.' (2) When we reject the whole value-system within which the given judgement is interpreted. (3) When it is impossible to find within the given value-system a principle which could justify the judgement; e.g., 'It is good to show magnanimity to slaves' within Aristotle's ethics.

Thus, value-judgements meet the postulate of controvertibility; that is, for any given value-judgement we can indicate conditions under which it may be proved false.

14.5 The cognitive content of a value-judgement may be of three kinds:

(a) accessible to those who know the value-language in whose terms a given judgement has been formulated,

(b) accessible to all knowing the given national language,

(c) indirectly contained in the judgement.

The line between (a) and (b) is fluid, and depends on the degree to which one knows the given value-language and national language.

(a) Interpreted on the basis of the given value-language, a judgement contains the information that the person, object, or act mentioned meets or does not meet certain criteria of evaluation. These criteria have to be empirically explicable, otherwise the statement will be incomprehensible. When an Athenian in the fourth century B.C. hears the judgement 'Nikias is a good man', he knows that Nikias is a free-born man, physically fit, healthy, active as a citizen. A thirteenth century Frenchman, told that 'In his fight with Alain, Jean showed himself a coward', learns that Jean is an unworthy man who fled from an armed adversary, his equal in social status. A seventeenth-century Puritan reading in a letter from Amherst, 'John Smith behaved badly last Sunday', learns that John Smith broke one of the strict rules prescribing behaviour on a holy day—for instance, he played his flute. To an eighteenth-century sentimentalist the judgement 'Virginia is a tender girl' expresses a highly positive assessment, from which he can deduce that she sighs when listening to music, likes to talk about doves and lambs, weeps when she hears about love.

The fact that anyone, who understands the given value-language, can on the basis of a description of certain facts formulate their appropriate evaluation, testifies to the presence of cognitive content in value-judgements. If in the four examples cited we take as the point of departure what we recognize as the cognitive content of evaluative judgements, we shall arrive at the same judgements.

The information about meeting or not meeting the specific criteria of assessment is, then, concrete information, facilitating the recognition of the evaluated object. But the cognitive content of a judgement is not limited to that. When evaluating, we implicitly form a class of objects, comparable from the point of view of the given value or criterion and arrange them so that the object evaluated is assigned a definite position within the implied class.

Evaluating someone as 'honest', 'intelligent', 'lazy', 'merciful', at the same time designates kinds of behaviour, or features of personality, and places the evaluated person on the scale of comparison determined by the applied value-system.

14.6 (b) If someone does not know the given value-language, for instance if he is unaware that in ancient Athens being free-born and healthy were prerequisites of being good, or that for the chivalric morality fleeing from even an obviously stronger enemy was a disgrace, or that for Puritans Sunday was a day devoted to thinking about God, then the cognitive content of a value-judgement will 'split', as described above (§14.3). On the one hand, one will understand the evaluative sense of the most general evaluative predicates without knowing the criteria on the basis of which they are predicated; on the other hand, one will understand the descriptive reference of other evaluative predicates without being sure of their evaluative import. In a word, in the understanding of the content of judgement there will occur a hiatus, corresponding to the popular differentiation between 'description' and 'evaluation'.

I have already said that this differentiation is historically and culturally relative (§5.11). This thesis can now be amplified. At times, and in axiologically homogeneous environments, i.e., where there is only one relatively coherent value-system, and one value-language, the connection between evaluation and its empirical criteria is comprehensible to every one. Description implies evaluation, evaluation implies description, and there is no chasm between them. At times and in spheres of cultural stability, and especially when and where vertical social mobility remains minimal, as in the Middle Ages, and also in social groups displaying a strong cohesiveness—as in Puritan settlements, court circles at the time of absolutism, in rural communities up till the end of the nineteenth century—description and evaluation are inseparable.

Most human societies known to us appear to have developed usually from simple and uniform to more complex and variegated structures. Such an impression is strengthened by the fact that written documents have been left only by and mostly about the educated classes. In pace with the historical diversification of societies the links between empirical criteria and evaluative verdicts in the consciousness of people using the same national language slowly loosen. Eighteenth-century individualism, particularly that inspired by Rousseau, speeded up and intensified this process, which has led to the present tangly situation. It is probably no accident that the doctrine of a gap between description and evaluation was formulated for the first time by a leading liberal philosopher of the mid-eighteenth century; nor that the end of the nineteenth, with its progressing socio-cultural disintegration, produced the beginnings of philosophical inquiry into the general theory of value and the logic of evaluative judgements.

But even if the axiological foundations of a given value-judgement remain hidden, information about the relative position occupied by the appraised object within the framework of an (unknown) value-system may be quite important, for this position determines the relation of the object to other analogous objects. The information about it may be not *stricto sensu* descriptive (see §5.2), but still we learn from it something factual, similarly as we learn from predicates like 'older', or 'edible'. 'John is older than Joseph' does not say anything about either John or Joseph taken separately, but gives information about the relation of their ages. Of course, the criteria of seniority are universal, but this is not relevant here. The criteria of edibility are far from being universal: the scope of edible things is larger in France than in Poland—Poles do not consider snails and frogs edible; and larger in Poland than in England—Poles thrive on sour milk and eat, apart from mushrooms, many other species of fungi. If we do not know the gastronomic habits of a people, we are unable to identify objects which they call 'edible'; but knowing French we could understand what position is occupied within the practical classification used by the French by objects called '*mangeable*'. Analogously, the statement 'Andrew is a good man', heard on the lips of somebody of whose value-system we are ignorant, does not tell us much about Andrew, but informs us of the position allotted to Andrew among other men. And such information is not negligible, since value-judgements are only rarely an expression of personal assessment, and usually reflect opinions, prevailing in social groups, ideological movements, and the like.

Thus a lack of understanding of a given value-language does not prevent us from obtaining a fairly important part of the information contained in an evaluative judgement, provided that we know the given national language.

14.7 (c) The indirect cognitive content of a value-judgement may be put in the form of a hypothesis about the probable consequences of the given kind of behaviour, or probable reactions to the given object or quality. A non-axiological example will illustrate the point. While driving a car, we notice a 'Stop' sign at an intersection. If we remember the highway code, we know that this sign demands that we stop the vehicle before moving on; we also know that such signs are positioned before intersections with main and faster roads, and at unguarded railway crossings. If we do not know the highway code, it is sufficient to understand the word 'stop' itself to learn that we had better apply the brakes. These are the two kinds of content which a 'Stop' sign can communicate to us directly. And indirectly the sign signals what may be the consequence of disobeying it: a police ticket, a collision, loss of our driving licence, and so on.

The same holds true in the case of value-judgements. Principles and criteria of evaluation are theoretical formulae, rules which may be set down on paper—but which empirically exist only in so far as there are people who put these principles and criteria to work, i.e., who think and behave in a certain manner. The value-principle 'Killing is evil' is externally experienced by us in this way that we and other people behave in a certain manner with respect to the acts of depriving men of their lives. The criterion of evaluation according to which an individual is lying, if he knows that x is the case but consciously maintains that x has never happened, remains a theoretical abstraction as long as someone does not say that the individual who denies x is a liar.

Thus, value-judgements signal the probability that certain specific socio-psychological situations will occur. The judgement 'Charles is a thief' indirectly contains the information that men will react in a particular manner to Charles's person; the judgement 'y was a noble act' indirectly informs us about the probable reaction to that act. The indirect cognitive content of judgements concerning fidelity to friends will be about sympathy and trust; of judgements concerning a merchant's honesty, about credit and customers.

Even if we leave aside the by no means negligible region of values 'institutionalized' in laws, rituals, and professional codes, we may generally note that evaluation, both in the sense of experience and of reasoning, is a social phenomenon. As Mannheim succinctly put it,

Valuations of human attitudes and activities . . . are originally set by groups. The more one goes back into history the more it becomes evident that the real carrier of standards is not the individual, but the group of which he happens to be the exponent. . . . Valuation is originally not an isolated psychological act of an individual, and for the most part cannot be explained in terms of subjective intention . . ..[1]

The social grounding of ethical values is of particular import. Not only because ethics is unthinkable without the existence of several individuals of the same species, but primarily because it is impossible to describe and analyse moral values and norms without taking into account their social implications. Apart from sociologists and cultural anthropologists, experimental psychologists, such as Piaget,[2] also present ample evidence that value-principles are a product and a function of social intercourse. A value-judgement never appears in a void; it is always a reaction to something and, if expressed, communicates its content in a concrete situation. It is, therefore, itself a moral—or political, ideological, aesthetic—act, and part and parcel of the axiological fibre of human activity.

The social character of ethical, and also cultural, evaluation strengthens the significance of the indirect cognitive content of value-judgements. It is notable that many predicates which function evaluatively, refer immediately to the reaction evoked by the evaluated object or act: 'moving', 'repellent', 'attractive', 'charming'.

The indirect cognitive content of value-judgements has a particular importance for those ethical theories which base all value on the practical consequences of the evaluated behaviour—such as hedonism, utilitarianism, evolutionism. This is apparently

[1] K. Mannheim, *Essays in Sociology and Social Psychology*, pp. 236–7.
[2] J. Piaget, *The Moral Judgement of the Child*, transl. M. Gabain (New York, 1962).

why the idea that value-judgements are, in one way or another, connected with predictions has been repeatedly put forth by contemporary philosophers affiliated to pragmatism. Dewey was the most vocal proponent of that idea.[1] Normative statements are sometimes also considered to be linked to predictions of success or reprisal. It is not quite clear, however, what role is played here by the multiplicity of meanings of 'ought'.[2] An obvious difficulty, presented by the prediction idea, consists in the fact that it is not easy to explain how a prognosis can be 'contained' in the value-judgement. The view proposed here has it that hypothetical predictions are naturally associated with value-judgements, that they form their indirectly communicated content.

14.8 Value-principles do not directly express any cognitive content, but communicate it only indirectly. Taken directly, the principle 'It is good always to tell the truth' says nothing about any facts. Indirectly, however, it is associated with a hypothesis that telling the truth will always produce desirable effects. Within evaluative systems already established and crystallized in social consciousness, the hypotheses apply to the actual results of the assessed acts and to the customary reactions to them. Within systems not yet implemented, proposed and preached by missionaries, moral reformers, prophets, and revolutionary ideologues, the hypotheses refer to imagined consequences.

What happens when a hypothesis, indirectly communicated in a value-judgement, turns out to be false? This cannot have any bearing on the truth of the judgements, because the hypothesis does not belong to its content. 'Gregory did wrong in bribing the judge' is a true judgement—or a false one, depending on the value-language within which interpreted—irrespective of the consequences of Gregory's act. However, if a hypothesis, usually associated with value-judgements of a certain kind, proves always

---

[1] See C. I. Lewis, *An Analysis of Knowledge and Valuation*, p. 372; A. Kaplan, 'Some Limitations of Rationality', in *Rational Decision*, ed. C. J. Friedrich (New York, 1964), pp. 55–64; J. Dewey, *The Quest for Certainty* (New York, 1929), pp. 260–3.

[2] G. Lundberg, 'Semantics and the Value Problem', *Social Forces* (1948), p. 114: '. . . all "should" or "ought" statements, as well as scientific statements, represent an expectation which is, in effect, a prediction.'

or frequently false, a tendency to question the whole value-system arises. The trust in the hitherto accepted values faces a crisis. Doubts of the faithful concerning the mercifulness and benevolence of God, doubts amongst humanitarians whether honesty always breeds a reciprocal reaction—these are simple instances of the process just mentioned. Perhaps the most immediate and common reaction to such fallibility of hypotheses is ordinary cynicism.

The end result of losing faith in the hypotheses associated with certain value-judgements is a rejection of the value-principles on which these judgements rest. Such a rejection renders these judgements false within the value-system accepted by the given individual or group. Thus, the indirect cognitive content of value-judgements has an indirect bearing on the potential truth or falsity of these judgements.

14.9 The cognitive content of value-judgements, both direct and indirect, possesses a strong motivational appeal. As Abraham Kaplan says, 'the possibility is even open that they can perform the normative function well only if they have cognitive meaning, and if in that meaning they are true, or somehow "presuppose" true propositions'.[1]

For those who understand the given value-language the motivational function of the directly communicated cognitive content of a value-judgement rests on the relative weight of the information about the position occupied by the evaluated object within the hierarchy of values of the given system. Of course, the motivational import will be different for a person who does not only know but also accepts the value-principle by which the said judgement is justified, from what it will be for a person who is cognizant of the system but rejects its principles. To understand a value-language and to accept the value-system expressed in it are two separate things. We may see the arguments of both Antigone and Creon, but approve of only one or neither of them.

The motivational impact of the cognitive content of a value-judgement on those who do not understand the given value-language is by and large a matter of coincidence. Such predicates

---

[1] A. Kaplan, 'Logical Empiricism and Value Judgements', in *The Philosophy of Rudolph Carnap*, ed. P. A. Schilpp (New York, 1963), p. 831.

as 'good', 'decent', 'vile', and the like can undoubtedly convey some information to anyone knowing English; however, if one does not know the value-system with which one should connect them in the given judgements, their motivational influence will depend on general associations and conditional reflexes. Similarly, when we overhear some unknown men address one of their number as 'boss', and we do not know whether that 'boss' is the chief of a gang, the head of an accounting office, or a former sergeant of a fire brigade, then although the word 'boss' informs us of the relative position of the man thus addressed, our attitude towards him will be a matter of accidental circumstances.

The indirect cognitive content of value-judgements, although it is frequently elusive and ambiguous, may exert a powerful motivational influence. The more distinctly the hypothesis concerning the reaction to or consequences of a certain act imprints itself in the minds of people, and the higher the degree of probability ascribed to this hypothesis, the stronger its motivational appeal. An institutionalization of values and a general cultural stabilization further the expected probability of hypothesis. But the urge for and anticipation of a major change of social and political situation may, as in the case of revolutionary movements, greatly bolster the expectations that the prediction will be fulfilled, and thus increase the motivational force of a judgement concerning, say, a 'new justice'. Most clearly predictive, of course, are judgements with predicates which may be called 'promissory'—like the above mentioned (§14.6) 'moving', 'pleasant', 'happy', 'repulsive'— which refer directly to the results of an action or to reactions to the evaluated object or person. Most aesthetic predicates belong in this category.

The motivational impact of both kinds of cognitive content of value-judgements is an important factor in the process of inculcating values and also norms bound to those values. It not only causes the development of certain behavioural patterns, but popularizes given ways of categorizing experience.

The relative significance of information carried directly and indirectly by value-judgements depends to a large degree on the type of a given value-system. If the system has the character of a codex, i.e., if its principles are binding irrespective of the possible

practical consequences of their implementation—as is the case in
many systems based on religion, or in the ethics of honour—then
motivationally the more important is the direct cognitive content of
a judgement, relating to the fulfilment or non-fulfilment of the
codex's postulates. If, however, the principles of the system are
based on the expected consequences of behaviour—as in utilitarianism and all kinds of what G. E. M. Anscombe calls 'consequentialism'[1]—then the indirect cognitive content comes to the fore.
Among other reasons, it is the rapid development, since the
eighteenth century, of the 'consequentialist' system which has
popularized among philosophers the tendency both to under-
estimate, or even ignore, the cognitive content expressed directly
by value-judgements, and also to play down the informative
function of these judgements. But I think it would be rash to
consider the spread of 'consequentialism' an irreversible process.

§15. *The cognitive content of aesthetic value-judgements*

15.1 Of all kinds of value judgements, it is the aesthetic which give
philosophers most trouble—or malicious satisfaction. Trouble to
those who wish to show that the content of value-judgements may
be a subject of rational discussion; satisfaction to those who regard
valuation as an expression of feelings, habits, and irrational
attitudes. Some axiologists try to avoid the predicament by strictly
separating and contrasting aesthetic and ethical evaluative judgements, and relegating the first to the sphere of taste about which,
apparently, *non disputandum est*.[2]

Are differences between the structures of ethical and aesthetic
evaluation so great as to render impossible the application of the
same concepts and analytic methods to both kinds of value-judgements? Although we cannot investigate this problem very
thoroughly, we cannot bypass it either. Let us examine briefly,
one by one, the principal differences between evaluative reasoning
in ethics and in aesthetics.

[1] *Is/Ought Question*, p. 187.
[2] See, e.g., S. Hampshire, 'Logic and Appreciation', in *Aesthetics and
Language*, ed. W. Elton (Oxford, 1954), pp. 161-9. Professor Hampshire lists
most of the arguments commonly raised against the meaningfulness of a
logical analysis of aesthetic evaluations.

(a) The importance of value-principles, i.e., of the general rules of evaluation, is greater in ethics than in aesthetics. When defending ethical evaluations, we refer to general assumptions more often than when we discuss aesthetic appraisals.

(b) Actions subject to ethical evaluation are regarded as repeatable and comparable in their basic aspects; works of art and, generally, all aesthetic objects are frequently considered unique and unrepeatable.

(c) Ethical judgements apply exclusively to rational beings and their actions; aesthetic judgements not only to a great variety of human products, but also to natural objects and occurrences.

(d) We are distinctly aware of the links between given ethical judgements, opinions, and decisions, and general philosophical, political, and social beliefs; in the case of aesthetic judgements, opinions, and preferences, such a connection seems tenuous.

(e) When we talk about the relativity of ethical evaluations (within a given value-system, and not comparatively) we have in mind other determinants than when we talk of the relativity of aesthetic appraisals. In the former case we have to do mainly with bio-psychological factors, such as sex, age, health, level of consciousness; in the latter, with historical ones, such as time or style.

(f) Ethical judgements, as Bentham noted, rest frequently on negative preferences, like shunning pain; aesthetic evaluations are always based on positive preferences; an aesthetic attitude aims always at achieving something, not at avoiding something.

Thus the differences—and there are probably more of them—are quite evident. But do they preclude a common analytic approach and terminology? Let us consider their implications.

(a) The practical consequences of divergences and incoherencies in ethical evaluation are incomparably more serious than is the case with aesthetic appraisals. Aesthetic evaluations only rarely form a basis of a decision; ethical ones do so frequently. Hence the stress on the coherence and predictability of the moral evaluations of given men and societies, and the resulting tendency to apply general rules as widely as possible. However, the fact that the consequences of disagreement in aesthetic matters are usually less important does not mean that men do not strive to avoid and settle such disagreements. If there were no chances of establishing some mutually comprehensible and acceptable rules and criteria of judgement, discussion of aesthetic matters would be largely a futile exercise in exchanging verbal gasps and shudders. But we do try to communicate and agree on aesthetic issues, and frequently we succeed. The mildness of practical consequences of disagreements, and a weaker ideological determination of aesthetic opinions allow for the coexistence of a greater number of value-systems in aesthetics than in ethics. It does not follow, however, that there are no general rules within these systems.

(b) Strictly speaking, no human action of the kind which is subject to moral evaluation is repeatable. In comparison to aesthetic objects the difference can only be quantitative, not qualitative. 'Uniqueness' and 'unrepeatableness' as applied to aesthetic objects are terms with more than one meaning. Perhaps most frequently they apply not to an allegedly fundamental feature of an aesthetic object, but to one of the possible criteria of judgement. And human behaviour or personality is also sometimes assessed in terms of 'exceptionality' and 'uniqueness'.

(c) The reach of aesthetic evaluations is enormous indeed, but human obstinacy in applying one name to all of them is, perhaps, a symptom of the existence of a common, integrative point of view. Similarly: the objects of different cults are greatly variegated but, because of a similarity of human attitudes towards them, we call all these objects 'religious'.

(d) The lack of close links between aesthetic opinions and a *Weltanschauung*—a phenomenon which is, by the way, of fairly recent origin—may justify a liberal and tolerant approach to aesthetic doctrines, but does not have to produce philosophical anarchy within aesthetics. The fact that the viability of aesthetic theories and evaluations does not necessarily hinge upon the acceptance of certain more general assumptions does not compel us to believe that these theories may be freely adopted without any broader philosophical premisses and implications.

(e) The historical and cultural determinants mentioned place aesthetic evaluations firmly within given historical and social contexts, and point to the fact that these evaluations are not simply expressions of accidental and individually isolated reactions.

(f) The positive 'unity of direction' of aesthetic appraisals constitutes a unifying element of aesthetic value-judgements. One might even be tempted to venture a hypothesis that, at least within the scope of European cultural traditions, men tend to treat with equal suspicion moral values openly and exclusively bound to the idea of pleasure, and aesthetic values shoving pleasure into the background. But a moment of reflection suffices to realize that in this respect also borderlines are fluid and differences a matter of degree.

We may conclude that there are no theoretically insurmountable obstacles to apply analogous analytic concepts to both the aesthetic and the ethical value-judgements. And there are weighty arguments for a unity of treatment; theoretical—since various kinds of evaluation are intertwined and separating them would be artificial and difficult; practical—since a strict fragmentation of human spiritual activities would have to be forced and crippling.

15.2 We have seen (§11.3) that the differentiation of types of value is a question which can be presented and solved only in historical terms, and that the lines between values run differently depending on the given value-system. This does not, however, necessitate our resigning any attempt at discovering the core of the aesthetic. Hitherto I have been talking about aesthetic value-judgements in terms of their conventional, intuitive identification. But we cannot proceed to an analysis of the cognitive content of these judgements without first answering the question: what marks them apart from other types of value-judgement? On what foundations can we rest our intuitions? Or, at least, where should we look for the differentiating element of the aesthetic? Given the present state of knowledge, an answer to this question can be formulated only in a tentative fashion.

The scope of 'the aesthetic', historically and socially changing, seems to be most clearly demarcated by means of the concept of an aesthetic attitude, or rather, a family of aesthetic attitudes. The notions of aesthetic experience and object would be derivative: an aesthetic experience is one made possible by adopting an aesthetic attitude; an object, towards which such an attitude is taken, becomes an aesthetic object.

The stable elements of the historically and socially variable aesthetic attitude are best characterized from the 'outside', namely by asking the question: what is the place of this attitude within the whole structure of human mental activity? Psychological, historical, and anthropological data indicate that the aesthetic lies between attitudes magical and religious on the one hand, and purely sensual on the other. The family of aesthetic attitudes neighbours on the one side the family of mystical and transcendental attitudes, on the other side the family of sensual and erotic attitudes.[1] Aesthetic attitudes may take two different polar forms, most easily discernible when the aesthetic object is a work of art. They may be close either to the pole of 'pure' sensual experiences, or to the pole of semantic interpretations; in other words, to the pole of sensations or to the pole of meanings.[2] It is symptomatic of this family of attitudes that links between the two poles, between the transcendental and sensuality, are always preserved;[3] and also that men adopting aesthetic attitudes are frequently conscious of their freedom to oscillate between these by no means mutually exclusive extremes. It is rather this freedom, and not any 'distance', which looks like an essential internal factor of the aesthetic attitude. The

[1] The origins of art are usually traced back to the vicinity of one of these poles. See, e.g., E. Grosse, *Die Anfänge der Kunst* (Freiburg and Leipzig, 1894); A. Hauser, *The Social History of Art* (New York, 1957), vol. i, pp. 1–11; L. J. Lafleur, 'Biological Evidence in Aesthetics', *Philosophical Review* (1942); H. Lhote, *Peintures préhistoriques du Sahara* (Paris, 1958); S. Ossowski, 'Z dociekań nad genezą sztuki', *Wiedza i Życie* (1938). Also W. James, *The Varieties of Religious Experience*, Ch. XIX. A combination of both hypotheses of origin is supported by K. Lorenz: 'all human art primarily developed in the service of rituals', *On Aggression* (London, 1967), p. 164.

This should not be understood as contradicting N. Goodman's thesis that the aesthetic attitude is close to the cognitive (*Languages of Art*, Indianapolis, 1968, pp. 241–52). On a low level of cultural sophistication, cognitive curiosity manifests itself within both the sensual and the magical, and in further development it does not sever these links. To imply that the aesthetic attitude is nowadays close to the scientific one would mean demanding altogether too much from the average consumer of aesthetic goods.

[2] This polar division is traversed by another one: into art interpreted as imitative—which can be both sensuous and mystical—and art interpreted as symbolical—which, as in the case of many abstract paintings, can be sensuous.

[3] See, e.g., light as a symbol of deity, and its sensuous role; red as colour and as a suggestion of blood, expensive pigment, social status. Good examples of the inseparability and interchangeability of functions are given by F. Sibley, 'Aesthetics and the Looks of Things', *Journal of Philosophy* (1951), pp. 909–15.

concept of aesthetic attitude, as sketched above, could be tested and more precisely formulated within psychology and cultural anthropology.

15.3 Within various systems of aesthetic evaluation many different values may coexist. Sometimes, as in the title of H. Osborne's *Theory of Beauty*, the term 'beauty' is taken to be synonymous with 'aesthetic value'. This, however, results in many ambiguities and confusions, since such an identification can be substantiated neither by the history of aesthetic concepts (see the distinction between 'the sublime' and 'the beautiful'), nor by current semantic intuitions. We do not hesitate to call paintings of Titian or Cézanne 'beautiful', but we have doubts whether to apply the same word to positively evaluated paintings of Matthias Grünewald or Max Ernst. Ugliness may be aesthetically valuable, but to say that ugliness may be beautiful sounds somewhat bizarre. Thus it is more convenient to reserve 'beauty' as the name of one of the kinds of aesthetic value.

To different aesthetic values correspond different sets of evaluative criteria. We have to distinguish various values appearing within different value-systems, and various values coexisting within one and the same system. The basic type of evaluative criteria may be classified as follows (this is intended as a meta-systemic classification, applicable to any system of aesthetic evaluation).

(a) According to the *kind* of *aesthetic object*: poems or sculptures, musical compositions or films, flowers or landscape paintings. A comprehensive—and open—typology of aesthetic objects cannot be limited to the traditional branches of the arts and to the so-called aesthetic categories, but must include natural objects and products of technology. The diversification of criteria is gradual: some are applied to literature rather than to the visual arts, others to sculpture rather than painting, while yet others are applicable to portraits in contrast to still life paintings.

(b) According to the *approach*, either *sensuous* or *semantic*.[1] Approaching an aesthetic object sensuously we concentrate our

---

[1] These are, I repeat, two approaches, and not two distinct kinds of aesthetic objects; even works of literature may be approached 'purely sensuously'.

attention on directly perceived qualities: colours, sounds, shapes, dimensions, sequences, the light in a landscape, the surface of a sculpture, the texture of a canvas. This approach is sometimes called, rather misleadingly, 'formalistic'. The semantic approach consists in connecting whatever is perceived with something else, signified or exemplified by it: interpreting the irregular shapes on a de Staël painting as football players, understanding the linguistic parodies in Joyce's *Ulysses*, recognizing Moses in a bearded figure and a human head in an oblong stone, realizing what are the functions of a given building, associating the finale of Beethoven's Ninth with joy or directly with Schiller's poem, interpreting the peacock on *The Adoration of the Magi* by Fra Angelico and Filippo Lippi as a symbol of immortality, connecting abstract shapes on Mondrian's paintings with the idea of a general order of the universe.

The adoption of a semantic approach is not determined by the origin of the given aesthetic object. We can approach semantically both human-made and natural objects. Sunsets and sundowns, kinds of weather, trees, flowers, and mountains are often treated as so-called 'natural signs'; this was a favoured speciality of the Romantics. Lévi-Strauss argues that a semantic approach to the surrounding reality is natural to the 'savage' man.[1] It is no wonder, then, that so many natural objects—eagles, asses, and oaks, green leaves and torrential waters, have been used as symbols since time immemorial and it is even difficult to approach them in a purely sensuous manner.

To these two poles within the family of aesthetic attitudes correspond two different, but still partly overlapping, groups of values and criteria. It is possible to evaluate a certain aesthetic object negatively from the semantic point of view, because we consider it muddled or boring, but to evaluate positively its sensuous aspect. This happened, for instance, in the revival of the art of Gustave Moreau. And vice versa: as the old puzzle of the 'aesthetic of ugliness' indicates, objects and elements sensuously repellent and jarring may be positively evaluated when the semantic approach is applied and when they are interpreted as signs or groups of signs.

---

[1] C. Lévi-Strauss, *La Pensée sauvage*, pp. 33–41, and *passim*.

This aesthetically relative role of signs was for the first time noticed apparently by Campanella.[1]

(c) Depending on whether we look for *artistic* or *experiential* values. This distinction is a very important one for aesthetics.[2]

Broadly speaking, artistic values pertain to the mutual relations of aesthetic objects, experiential values to the relations between aesthetic objects and their perceivers. The artistic value-principles offer ultimate justification to judgements and preferences concerning artistic skills, techniques, and devices, and also historical and structural relations between works of art, which, among other things, reveal the presence or absence of the so-called creative element. Sometimes we apply artistic criteria also to the evaluation of natural objects, as when we talk about an original hue in blue carnations, the unusual shape of a certain species of orchids, the unique landscape of the Grand Canyon of the Colorado, or about the forms of mountain crystals, and harmonious patterns of optical spectra.

The experiential value-principles justify judgements pertaining to aesthetic experiences[3]—to what we feel and think when faced with an aesthetic object. To issue a judgement on the artistic value of an object it is unnecessary to have any immediate experience of that object. For instance, second-hand information about the prosodic structure and tropes of a poem may suffice to assess its originality or derivativeness. Experiential value is founded on the emotions and thoughts aroused in the subjects: serenity or indig-

[1] 'Quapropter nihil est quod non sit pulchrum simul et turpe', quoted by B. Croce, *Aesthetic*, transl. D. Ainslie (London, 1922), p. 171.

[2] A similar, if vaguer, classification was proposed by S. Ossowski: 'objects with which aesthetics deals we evaluate in some cases with respect to the experiences of their perceivers or listeners, in others with respect to the creative activity, which gave them birth'. '. . . these two methods of evaluation in aesthetics one may call, for short, evaluation with respect to beauty and evaluation with respect to artistry.' *U podstaw estetyki*, pp. 284, 285. R. Ingarden's differentiation of 'two categories of value', the 'artistic' and the 'aesthetic', is made on completely different grounds, although it partly overlaps with the classification proposed here. *Studia z estetyki*, vol. ii (Warsaw, 1958), pp. 104–11.

[3] I am using here 'experience' in a somewhat specialized sense, as equivalent to German 'Erlebnis' or Polish 'przeżycie' (literally: 'living through something').

nation, insight into the personalities of other men, the excitement of analysis and discovery, an enriched vision of the world, thoughts about the tragedy of existence, of human loneliness and solidarity.

When we say that a painting is original, a play a plagiarism, that a novel has fast action, a building is a mixture of styles, or that a symphony has influenced a whole generation of followers, we apply artistic concepts and criteria. An evaluation based on them does not have to concur with an evaluation based on experiential values. Gertrude Stein's *A Book Concluding as a Wife Has a Cow* is an influential and highly original piece, but aesthetically tedious; Shakespeare borrowed his plots from other authors; the Sienese Duomo is beautiful in spite of its mixture of styles; nineteenth-century academic painting, for many years so little valued aesthetically, is technically excellent.

Of course, both kinds of value are closely interrelated. We apply the criteria of artistic value that we do because we assume that the results of the qualities so chosen will be experientially satisfacory; we evaluate works of art experientially using artistic categories of style, convention, trend, or motif. 'Style' is perhaps the best example of an artistic term enormously important for aesthetic experience and evaluation.[1]

(d) According to whether we evaluate *individual* aesthetic objects, or *species* of aesthetic objects.

Aesthetic objects are usually evaluated as belonging to a given class: lyrical poems, Westerns, mountain landscapes, symphonies. But questions may also be asked: is a good thriller as valuable as a good tragedy? A good historical painting as a good still life? A beautiful landscape as a beautiful cathedral? Ancient Greeks valued string music more highly than flute music; various cultural trends would put on their pedestals different literary genres—epic, tragedy, pastoral, novel—or kinds of painting—interiors, landscapes. Whether Art is more beautiful than Nature was for many years a subject of serious debate.

When we appraise particular aesthetic objects we apply criteria —semantic or sensuous, artistic or experiential—appropriate to the

[1] An excellent discussion of the problems connected with the definition and theory of style is M. Schapiro's 'Style', in *Anthropology Today*, pp. 287–312.

class to which we allocate the given object. But when we compare the value of whole genres or species we apply criteria of a different sort. They may be artistic in character: we juxtapose the difficulty of producing works of art of a given type, or the frequency with which the given kind of natural objects appear. Most often, however, we compare classes of aesthetic objects from the point of view of the *type of experience* they usually produce. We could even say that, roughly, evaluation within a species is usually one with regard to the intensity of the ensuing experience, and evaluation of a species is one with regard to the quality of that experience. This is what the Greeks did, and what people do now who rank the experiences induced by a tragedy above those induced by a melodrama; those to which a philosophical novel gives rise above those produced by historical romances; those by figurative painting higher than those produced by abstract painting.

This fourth differentiation of aesthetic criteria is similar to the common opposition of 'serious' art and art as 'entertainment'. But these popular categories apply to works of art only, are vague and difficult to apply to the past. They are also burdened with élitism. It would be preferable to talk, even on the level of crude generalizations, about 'easy' and 'difficult' art.

15.4 Aesthetic judgements are conclusions of aesthetic evaluations —as experiences and as reasonings. A most important role in these evaluations is played by anticipation, i.e., the presuppositions and expectations that determine our approach to the given aesthetic object. (For ethical value-judgements a similar role is played by situational contexts, i.e., by the concrete physical and human circumstances, within which the evaluated fact appears.) Anticipation is a kind of attitude. It may involve, on the one hand, conscious expectations, and, on the other, habits, training, and associative dispositions.

What we perceive depends, to a large degree, on what we expect to perceive. This is a banal truth, but its implications are not always fully realized. Here are a few examples of the role of anticipation in cognition.

(a) Experiments in the physiology of vision have demonstrated that identifying shapes, even the very simple ones such as straight and curved lines, is made possible by the fact that after the first impulse has been registered on the retina, the eye continues scanning the scene in 'anticipation' of what the receptors on the surface of the retina are going to register. What is finally registered and transmitted as an 'image' to the brain is a self-congruence of consecutive stimuli. The more experienced the eye and the more precise the anticipation, the shorter time is needed to identify the shape.[1] In cases of incorrect anticipation one often gets an optical illusion.

(b) In his *Art and Illusion* Ernst H. Gombrich lists several illustrators—from the pre-photographic time—who, although certainly intending to give a faithful report of the objects represented, could not escape the influence of their own assumptions about what these objects *should* be like and drew not quite what there was in front of them but rather what they expected to see.[2] They were bound by the 'stereotypes' of vision, formed by strongly inculcated habits of anticipation.

(c) Anybody familiar with phonetics knows that an analysis of recordings of standard speech reveals strong deviations from the theoretical norms of language. But usually we understand even grossly distorted words, because we know what to expect. Similarly a reader not specifically alerted misses most of the minor misprints in the daily press, because he perceives printed words in the form he expects them to have.

(d) I. A. Richards writes: 'Equally where what is expected recurs and where it fails, all rhythmical and metrical effects spring from anticipation.'[3] That is, a poem appears to us to be prosodically organized or disorganized according to the expectations with which we read it.

What are the modes of anticipation pertaining to aesthetic objects? The following seem to be the most important.

(a) Anticipation corresponding to different kinds of aesthetic objects.

We expect one thing from poetry, another from architecture, something other from a landscape than from a symphony. To

---

[1] J. R. Platt, 'How we see Straight Lines', *Scientific American* (Jan. 1962), pp. 121–9.

[2] E. H. Gombrich, *Art and Illusion* (The Bollingen Foundation, New York, 1960), pp. 68–74.

[3] I. A. Richards, *Principles of Literary Criticism* (London, 1924), p. 134.

suppose that we expect experiences of the same sort from different kinds of aesthetic objects is like assuming that we feel the same kind of pleasure eating pears and herring, drinking brandy and milk.

(b) Anticipation resulting from the recognition of a style, genre, or, most generally, convention.

An opened book with pages printed evenly from left to right evokes different expectations from one in which we recognize verse, and different still from one which consists solely of dialogue. The subtitles 'tragedy' or 'farce', or an invocation to the Muses at the beginning of a poem, carry the suggestion of a specific convention. A glimpse of the ornate façade of a baroque or late Gothic church leads us to expect a different experience from that intimated by the sight of a simple classical fronton. When, opening a novel at random, we find a detailed description of the 'seamy side of life', we brace ourselves for a piece of naturalistic prose. Various and complex symptoms signal that a given work of art is symbolic; we do not approach such a work in the same way as a non-symbolic one.

(c) Anticipation consequent upon the knowledge of history.

Knowing art history facilitates and enriches aesthetic experience precisely because it arranges our expectations regarding distance in time, literary themes, the texture of works in the visual arts, the harmonic structure of pieces of music, the purpose of buildings.

(d) Anticipation of structural fulfilment.

Listening to a piece of music we expect that the initial theme will be developed and lead to a 'fulfilling' finale. Looking at a Gothic cathedral we expect to find a structural development of the basic scheme of arch and rosette. Reading works of 'easy' fiction, like detective stories, we anticipate a specific formal structure. The phenomenon of 'kitsch' consists primarily in the fact that the public knows very well what to expect both artistically and experientially, and is quickly satisfied. From this point of view L. B. Meyer's remarks are interesting. He believes that 'The differentia between art music and primitive music lies in the speed of tendency gratification.'[1] In other words, 'primitive' (the term which Meyer uses, somewhat misleadingly, as synonymous with banal and easy) music satisfies expectations promptly and without surprises.

[1] L. B. Meyer, 'Some Remarks on Value and Greatness in Music', *Journal of Aesthetics and Art Criticism* (June 1959), p. 494.

The anticipated regularity of structure does not have to imply banality; it may, as in classical art, form a conventional frame which in fact emphasizes thematic originality or structural innovations.

(e) Anticipation of a specific experience.

We may anticipate the kind of experience which a given aesthetic object is to produce. One may go to a picture gallery to enjoy the subtlety of colours, or to get an illusion of the ever-presence of the past, or to enrich one's knowledge of human character by looking at portraits. One may expect similar experiences from different aesthetic objects—e.g., a feeling of tranquility from a landscape, a lyrical poem, or a sonata; and different experiences from the same or similar aesthetic objects. One man reads *The Magic Mountain* looking for allegories of and disquisitions about time; another, searching for a symbolic presentation of two opposing political and moral ideals; another still, wanting to find a picture of the spiritual atmosphere in Europe in the years preceding the First World War An important role in creating this type of anticipation is played by the titles of works of art, which condition the attention of the public.

(f) Anticipation of novelty.

When we approach an aesthetic object that is unknown to us, we anticipate meeting with something in a significant way different from formerly encountered objects of the same kind: we expect something unexpected. This 'anticipated surprise' may consist in artistic originality in the piece, its themantic novelty, fresh ideas, or a unique pattern of colours and dimensions in a landscape. We assume that this surprise should lead to an aesthetic experience different from other familiar experiences.

We may put it the other way: the immediate recognition of originality in a work of art also rests on specific expectations, which are only partly fulfilled; the margin of unfulfilment forms the index of originality. This margin, understandably, cannot be too broad. As T. S. Eliot said, absolutely original poetry is absolutely bad.

(g) Ossified anticipation.

Critics of the arts, especially those who belong to an older generation, often approach new works of art with a habit of anticipation so rigid that they are incapable, not only of aesthetic experience, but even of understanding novel artistic structures and fresh themes—e.g., in impressionism, non-figurative painting, imaginist poetry, atonal music. An instance of ossified anticipation may be also the application of typological and analytic concepts, formed in a particular historical setting, to the description and interpretation of objects belonging to a different time and style. Late Roman, Gothic, baroque, mannerist, and primitive art were, in their turn, victims of such a treatment. Even Wölfflin's 'categories of representation', allegedly universal, turned out to be, in fact, classical. Kenneth Clark affords us a good example of ossified anticipation in the preface to the second edition of his *Gothic Revival*. After the publication of his book he realized that the criteria of judgement he applied to evaluation of neo-Gothic architecture were based on prejudice, originating in the dogmatic, anti-nineteenth-century opinions of contemporary critics.[1]

15.5 What are the implications of this manifold role of anticipation for the analysis of aesthetic value-judgements? Above all, it follows that anticipation constitutes an essential component of the context of both aesthetic experience and judgement. It gives a definite direction, one of many possible, to an aesthetic experience. The differences in appraisals of the same aesthetic objects may result not only from differences in value-systems, but also from differences in anticipation; and an aesthetic judgement may even be seen as true or false with respect, among other things, to the given expectations concerning the object of the judgement (see §15.7).

In those types of art whose works are preserved in the form of notation—in literature, music, drama, ballet—the aesthetic object itself is in each case of its being perceived shaped under the influence of certain expectations. A critic's job consists, to a large degree, in a suggestive attuning of our expectations to our experiences. He may do it in advance, or *ex post facto*. For instance, Lionel Trilling asks us to look back to our reading of *Mansfield Park* and teaches us to recognize shades of irony in Jane Austen which, unsuspected, may well have passed unnoticed.[2] In such a case we project our new expectations back on to our past experience. We know also how much it helps sometimes when we wish to

---

[1] K. Clark, *The Gothic Revival*, 2nd ed. (London, 1950), pp. 1–7.
[2] L. Trilling, *The Opposing Self* (London, 1955), pp. 206–30.

reach an agreement in evaluation just to reiterate our explanation of how to perceive the object in question.[1] This applies particularly to discerning structural elements in a painting, a composition, or a poem. The richer the scope of expectations concerning the given work of art, the more room there is for its varying interpretations and evaluations. The more limited and vague the expectations, the more accidental the aesthetic experience and the more poorly substantiated the evaluation. In the case of works transmitted in notation, and particularly works of literature, lack of definite expectations results in a hazy realization of the aesthetic object.

True, sometimes we encounter aesthetic objects which astonish us by their unexpected difference. Such astonishment may lead to a particularly vivid experience. But we have to distinguish between, on the one hand, astonishment conditioned by past acquaintance with objects of the same class and aesthetic surprise which we anticipate in any new aesthetic object, and, on the other hand, amazement or fascination with novelty which has little to do with aesthetic experience. The surprise in beholding an aesthetic object with completely unexpected qualities is more like the amazement felt when we find a hamster in our desk drawer than like the awareness of aesthetic novelty thrown into relief by more or less conscious anticipation.

We may also say that given expectations determine not only particular interpretation, but also specific sets of evaluative criteria. What we anticipate nearly always possesses for us a distinct value-quality—it is important, worthy, or despicable, but almost never indifferent. Therefore, if we know what is anticipated, we may predict the frame of interpretation and also the terms of judgement.

15.6 An aesthetic value-judgement can be regarded as true within the terms of a given value-language, if the facts mentioned in it are the case and if within the value system, expressed by that language, we are able to identify a value-principle on which the judgement may be founded.

When we know the given value-language, then from a judgement, understood within the context of that language, we may learn that the appraised object meets, or does not meet, the appropriate,

---

[1] See L. Wittgenstein, *Philosophical Investigations* II, xi (Oxford, 1953), pp. 200–2.

empirically recognizable criteria of aesthetic evaluation. Thus someone who has read Wordsworth's Preface to the *Lyrical Ballads* knows that a poem called 'beautiful' by a romanticist is intensely emotional, its heroes are simple people and/or supernatural beings, the language is fairly close to common speech with an admixture of provincialism, and so on. When we remember Burke's formula that beauty 'is a name I shall apply to such qualities in things as induce in us a sense of affection and tenderness, or some other passion the most nearly resembling these',[1] we understand the information passed in their judgements by the late eighteenth-century sentimentalist critics.

Of course, for an object to be assessed as aesthetically valuable it is not enough that it possess the requisites named by a value-principle. It is also assumed, usually tacitly, that it meets many other requirements. A poem must not be too long or rhythmically inept; a painting was until recently supposed to depict some object, etc. These prerequisites, some physiological in origin (e.g., limitations in sound frequency and volume) and some characteristic of particular traditions and value-systems, are most commonly negative in form: 'unless it is . . .'; they do not, however, change the basic links between value-judgements and value-principles.

When one does not know the given value-language, one simply does not understand why a certain sculpture is said to be 'beautiful', a sonata 'marvellous', or a comedy 'miserable'. Moreover, one does not know whether, e.g., 'realistic', 'tender', or 'romantic' are used as evaluative or as descriptive predicates, and whether, if used evaluatively, they purport to express a positive or a negative appraisal. When the statement contains one of the general evaluative terms—such as 'good', 'beautiful', 'hideous'—we can guess that its utterer either himself has a positive, or negative, opinion about the given object, or reports of such an opinion held by some-

[1] E. Burke, *A Philosophical Inquiry into the Origin of our Ideas of the Sublime and Beautiful*, iii. 1. He goes on to list the 'sensible qualities' of beauty: 'First to be comparatively small. Secondly, to be smooth. Thirdly, to have a variety in the direction of the parts; but, fourthly, to have those parts not angular, but melted as it were into each other. Fifthly, to be of a delicate frame, without any remarkable appearance in strength. Sixthly, to have its colours clear and bright, but not very strong and glaring. Seventhly, or if it should have any glaring colour, to have it diversified with others.'

body else. But positive and negative aesthetic opinions may be held for widely divergent reasons. This is why in criticism it is essential to combine description and evaluation, especially in periods when many aesthetic tendencies coexist. Describing a given work of art or fragment of nature and interspersing his description with terms carrying an evaluative undertone—like 'quiet', 'harmonious', 'coherent', 'dynamic', 'deep', 'clear'—a critic leads us to comprehend his criteria for judgement, and signals what connections he sees between empirical properties, reactions to them, and the value ascribed to the object presented. Thus his description sets in front of us a piece of his value-system. Listing the qualities which he considers aesthetically significant, a critic reveals his standards of judgement and declares: this is what I regard as seminal and worthy, and that is what I regard as tedious and trite. Our contemporary plenitude of value-languages in aesthetics makes it necessary to demand from critics that they clearly state their axiological positions. Only if they do, are we able to say whether, to what extent, and why we agree, or disagree, with their judgements.

15.7 It was said above (§15.1) that value-principles in aesthetics are at least in one respect more homogeneous than in ethics: they all rest on a tacit assumption that the qualities of aesthetic objects, named in a value-principle, tend to evoke a positive aesthetic reaction. This characteristic of aesthetic values influences the type of cognitive content of aesthetic appraisals; namely, in an aesthetic judgement its indirect cognitive content is particularly important. It may be encapsulated in the form of a hypothesis, or prediction, about the probable reaction to the given aesthetic object on the part of persons belonging to a certain cultural milieu implied by the context of the judgement, and holding presuppositions analogous to those which formed the point of departure of the judgement in question.

The direct cognitive content of an aesthetic judgement is often difficult to pin down because of our inability to identify the value-system to which the given judgement belongs. But the prognosis, indirectly suggested by a judgement, attracts our attention immediately. When we read that Faulkner's *The Sound and the Fury* is a 'difficult masterpiece',[1] we may not know on what axiological ground the judgement rests and on which features of the book it is based, but we cannot doubt that the critic predicts an arduous but satisfying reading of the novel. 'Tender' or 'provocative' may have various evaluative functions, but it is clear what kinds of experience they foretell.

Thus a link between the content of aesthetic value-judgements and concrete experiences is apparent. One may say that a confrontation of values with facts is easier in aesthetics than in other fields of evaluation. Besides, empirical 'testing' of an aesthetic judgement may be practically complicated but it seldom presents a risk, apart from a loss of time. As indicated above, it is simpler to test the indirect than the direct cognitive content of aesthetic appraisals. And since most aesthetic value-systems are of the 'consequentialist' type, i.e., they found value-principles on the immediate results produced by beholding aesthetic objects, the indirect cognitive content is for aesthetic value-judgements singularly important and easily overshadows their direct sense.

Strictly speaking, a judgement is true or false, within the terms of a given value-language, only with respect to its direct content and irrespective of the situational context of its utterance. But culturally misplaced judgements, while theoretically true, may be contextually absurd. A Mississippi village school teacher, announcing to his pupils that *Ulysses* is a magnificent novel and that Georges Braque painted exquisite still lifes full of poetic charm, will probably have the direct cognitive content of his judgement misunderstood, and the indirectly expressed hypothesis proved false.

The above is, of course, an instance of cultural diversification, which is at least as much a matter of different values as of an alternative mode of anticipation (in any case, it is impossible to separate them empirically). A difference in presuppositions is bound up with a change in the denotation of terms, 'evaluative' as well as 'descriptive', used to render the resulting experiences. Depending on the nature of one's expectations, 'long', 'quiet', 'spacious', 'moody', 'turbulent', or 'simple' will denote different

---

[1] I. Howe, *William Faulkner* (New York, 1951), p. 158.

qualities in an aesthetic object. Therefore, if someone communicates an evaluation, based on a set of expectations U, to persons holding expectations W, he interjects alien terms[1] into the language used by everybody else and, although his statement may be theoretically true, it is practically false. This is the sense in which anticipation has a bearing on the truth and falsity of value-judgements.

Recognizing a value-judgement as false because it is 'misplaced', and also becoming disillusioned with the results of the prognosis obliquely contained in a given judgement, have both to be distinguished from deciding, on theoretical grounds, that a judgement is false. A schematic example will illustrate the point. Let us assume that we accept a value-system, which contains the principle that possessing the properties a, b, and c is a necessary and sufficient condition of being beautiful. The judgement 'X is beautiful' ought, within this system, to rest on the premiss that X possesses the properties a, b, and c. We deem this judgement false if it transpires that X does not in fact possess some, or any, of the listed properties.

But what happens if the hypothesis, indirectly communicated by this judgement and predicting that within the given cultural milieu people will admire X, turns out to be false in a large majority of cases? Most probably, there will emerge an irresistible tendency to throw the principle overboard. In other words, a frequent disillusionment with regard to prognoses leads to a change, not in particular assessments, but in the whole system of evaluation. The simplest and commonest example of such a process is the phenomenon of 'wearing-off' of artistic conventions. Widely accepted and popularized, they lose their original evocative force, become dull and ineffectual; the time comes for a general reassessment of style.

Cultural diversification is marked mainly by differences in what is anticipated and temporal change in aesthetics preferences is brought about chiefly by a fading of responses. Both phenomena are commonly referred to as differences in 'taste'. But 'taste' has

[1] A value-language may allow for a variety of expectations; thus a difference in expectations, and the resulting change in denotation of predicates, need not —although it may—constitute a difference in value language.

several meanings, some of which are notoriously vague. To make this term more definite it is perhaps useful to contrast it with 'anticipation'. A difference in preferences caused by a difference in anticipation would not, then, be a matter of taste; and a difference in preferences shown in conditions where the expectations remained the same would be either a matter of value-principles, or a matter of taste.

15.8 How do aesthetic value-judgements function on the motivational plane? What is their source and effect?

The question 'what makes x aesthetically valuable?' has to be distinguished from the question 'what makes A state that x is aesthetically valuable?' The former concerns a justification of the judgement, the latter an explanation of the motives for expressing it. And the motive for expressing an aesthetic judgement is often not a wish to communicate one's opinion, but rather a desire to persuade others to share it. A critic rarely acts as a judge pronouncing his verdict; usually he is a propagandist, an aesthetic preacher, even a prophet.

What is the basis of the motivational impact of aesthetic evaluations? In contrast to ethical or political evaluation, the direct cognitive content of aesthetic judgements, i.e., information concerning the position occupied by the evaluated object within the given value-system, has now only a weak motivative force. (Formerly, with a smaller number of aesthetic systems and a sharper differentiation between them, that force used to be much stronger.) By and large, the information that an aesthetic object fails to meet the standards of a given value-system does not by itself influence significantly our attitude towards it. This is so because the coherence of behaviour based on evaluation, so important in ethics that it sometimes becomes a value in itself, in modern aesthetics plays a diminishing role—which, in fact, arouses a justified anxiety as a symptom of a general disintegration of our 'world of values'. In the field of aesthetics we tend to strive at the richest possible variety of experience, and exhortations to consistency pass largely unheeded.

But while aesthetic judgements exert only a weak motivational force as appeals for orthodoxy, they function prominently as favourable or unfavourable forecasts. The promise, which they communicate indirectly, not only tempts us towards or repels us from becoming acquainted with given aesthetic objects, but also influences our expectations and *eo ipso* our future experiences. It has been correctly observed that the forecasts intimated by aesthetic appraisals fall in that class of 'self-fulfilling prophecies', because the fact of their being communicated furthers their realization. Thus the cognitive content, if only indirect, of aesthetic value-judgements is the basis of their motivational appeal.

15.9 I shall sum up the results of this section in the form of a brief analysis of a concrete instance of evaluative statement. Edmund Wilson, irked by the general adulation of Kafka, thus concluded his dissenting opinion:

If, however, one puts Kafka beside writers with whom he may properly be compared, he still seems rather unsatisfactory. Gogol and Poe were equally neurotic, in their destinies they were equally unhappy; and if it is true ... that there is present in Kafka's world neither personality nor love, there is no love in either Gogol or Poe, and though there are plenty of personalities in Gogol, the actors of Poe, as a rule, are even less characterized than Kafka's. But, though the symbols that these artists generate are just as unpleasant as Kafka's, though, like his, they represent mostly the intense and painful realization of emotional *culs-de-sac*, yet they have both certain advantages over Kafka—for Gogol was nourished and fortified by his heroic conception of Russia, and Poe, for all his Tory views, is post-Revolutionary American in his challenging, defiant temper, his alert and curious mind. In their ways, they are both tonic. But the denationalized, discouraged, disaffected, disabled Kafka, though for the moment he may frighten or amuse us, can in the end only let us down. He is quite true to his time and place, but it is surely a time and place in which few of us want to linger—whether as stunned and hypnotized helots of totalitarian states or as citizens of freer societies, who have relapsed into taking Kafka's stories as evidence that God's law and man's purpose are conceived in terms so different that we may as well give up hope of ever identifying the one with the other.[1]

There is only one straightforward value-judgement here: that Kafka is 'rather unsatisfactory'. Justifying it, the critic explains his criteria and reveals his value-principles: it is good to be 'tonic'; it is wrong to 'let the reader down'. Evidently, these are not purely

[1] E. Wilson, *Classics and Commercials* (New York, 1962), pp. 301–2.

aesthetic, but ethical–aesthetic principles. But in literary criticism, even in Anatole France's 'adventures of the soul among master-pieces', it is rare to encounter a clear separation of these two spheres.

The 'tonic' principle is bound to specific expectations, namely it is assumed that a work of fiction will influence its readers' attitude in life and boost their morale. Moreover, it is expected that the author adopt an active and critical, and not simply reflective, attitude towards the object of his artistic presentation. Wilson's approach is thoroughly semantical: he is interested in the most general sense of Kafka's work, and not in the rhythm of his cadences or the structure of his narratives. He applies criteria experiential as well as artistic (shaping of characters, symbols), and uses with relish that particular type of artistic criterion, which many theorists consider illegitimate, biographical con-siderations.[1]

Against Wilson's presuppositions we may set others; for example, one may expect of a novel the most faithful and immediate rendering of a situation and mood, without any critical comment or distance, with interpretation and judgement left fully to the reader. As long, however, as we remain on the ground demarcated by Wilson's value-system, the fundamental problem remains: tonic or not tonic? If Kafka is not tonic, but still somehow satisfies —for instance, because our expectations are different—then we shall be disposed to reject Wilson's value-principle and point out, e.g., that 'letting the reader down' may be valuable because it helps him shed illusions about the ideal order of the universe. And if it turns out that he *is* tonic—then we shall have to consider Wilson's judgement false: in the terms of his own principle, Kafka will appear satisfactory. We shall also reject, as misleading, the prognosis communicated in the judgement.

Whatever the result of our inquiry at the level of the theoretical

---

[1] It may seem odd that I consider the application of biographical criteria a species of investigating artistic value. This, however, is the only reasonable position. Biographical considerations do not relate directly to the experiences of readers, or perceivers in general, but offer a way of analysing works of art and their mutual relations by means of facts or, more frequently, suppositions concerning their authors.

pattern of evaluation, reading Wilson's criticism will surely have a motivational effect. It is at such an effect that the whole piece is carefully aimed. Comparing Kafka to Gogol and Poe, the critic appeals directly to our sensibilities. As a result, we shall certainly become better aware of the weakness and the strength of Kafka's passive pessimism.

CHAPTER IV

THE CHOICE OF VALUES

§16. *Validation of a choice of values*

16.1 The system of analytic concepts, presented in the three preceding chapters, is aimed not at an axiological neutralization of the philosophy of value, but at a modernization of its outfit. Terminological as well as methodological proposals are supposed to help in attaining this goal. Let us now consider, if only briefly and in the most general terms, the implications and the possibility of making use of the construed equipment.

First I shall list a few methods which may be helpful in arriving at a choice of values, and particularly in investigating and validating or disqualifying, the choice actually or hypothetically made. These methods supplement each other and partly overlap.

To choose between values one has to be aware of a possibility of choice, and have the practical ability to reach a conscious decision. For that it is necessary not only to have an active, not uncritical, attitude towards the existing situation, but also an ability to compare the values from among which a choice is feasible. If one attempts such a comparison using the terms of a particular value-system, e.g., presenting Christian ethics in the categories of utilitarianism, one implies an evaluation in the very process of description. This is why an analytic metalanguage has to be worked out. Only such a metalanguage, uncommitted to any of the competing value-systems, will permit a rational choice, one not forced solely by traditional prejudices and emotional promptings. This is the first way the philosophy of value may help in choosing values. Outlining the basic elements of such a metalanguage was one of the purposes of this work.

16.2 The second method consists in introducing a division of axiological labour: allotting particular tasks to specialists, and then analysing the results of their investigations.

How can that labour be divided? First, the philosopher may

concentrate on the theoretical pattern of evaluation and leave the motivational pattern to experts: psychologists, physiologists, sociologists, historians of culture. The origins and functioning of value-systems and particular judgements is a complex matter, requiring skills and techniques of research.

Secondly, the philosophers may, when investigating a given statement or a whole value-system, isolate and turn over to specialists particular assumptions and hypotheses which are capable of a direct empirical verification. Thus for instance the judgement that 'Michael did well not telling Mrs. Brown that her son had been killed' rests presumably on the premiss that a lasting uncertainty is less harmful for Mrs. Brown's health than the news that her son is dead (and health is here regarded as having a higher value than truth). A specialist may be able to verify this hypothesis. Similarly, a judgement which condemns the beating of children rests presumably not on the principle of parental love—as love does not rule out thrashing—but on the hypothesis that corporal punishment causes complexes. In the field of aesthetics the specialists' verification should cover all statements concerning artistic values; and problems such as 'understanding works of art' ought to be subdivided into questions concerning particular types of the arts and assigned to psychologists, sociologists, and theorists of art—only the results of their scrutiny can provide the philosopher with the appropriate data and allow him to avoid the grosser dangers of dilettantism.

Thirdly, the philosopher may formulate concrete questions which he considers pertinent for empirical axiology, with a view to bringing about a better understanding of the factual contexts of evaluative utterances. To such questions belong, e.g., the problem of the relation between population density and human behaviour, the dependence of fluctuation in aesthetic assessments on the frequency of perceptions, correspondence between psychological type and the type of values chosen. Much work of that kind has already been done.

16.3 The third method is one of reconstructing the reasoning required to justify a given judgement, and, vice versa, of revealing the theoretical implications of value-principles and general value-judgements. In this way, the philosopher exposes the theoretical structure of a given system of evaluation, erecting a 'ladder' of propositions, which reaches from particular judgements, through various stages of evaluations coupled with empirical statements, up to value-principles. He may investigate, for instance, what value-principles and empirical premisses are needed to justify the judgement asserting that it is good when exhibitions of painting are subsidized by public money. Or, how we pass from the principle of equality of all men to the negative appraisal of certain systems of education.

Construing and analysing the 'ladders' will have both a theoretical and a motivational function. On the theoretical level it will result in the arranging and better understanding of the operational or projected value-systems and will show their implications, hidden contradictions, mutual links and incompatibilities. It will be possible to determine what connections exist between certain metaphysical and ideological tenets, and value-principles associated with them. On the motivational level, a disclosure and presentation of the components of a system, and of its metaphysical underpinnings, will put that system to the test of one's beliefs, inclinations, and feelings.[1] The construction of a 'ladder' may prove to be an unmasking of the system—since men often do not know, or do not wish to know what are the foundations and implications of their values.[2]

An analysis of the structure of a system will also result in a confrontation, theoretically and motivationally momentous, of its two poles: value-principles and particular assessments. When hesitating between two conflicting judgements, one frequently relies on immediate and half-intuitive reactions and impulses, which may be accidental and uncontrolled, but possess the force of spontaneous naturalness. A choice between two value-principles is a

---

[1] See J. Ladd, *The Structure of a Moral Code*, p. 181: 'The appeal to existential grounds is the ultimate method by which the basic prescriptions of a system can be vindicated, and, perhaps, in some instances repudiated.'

[2] Methods similar to this and the next are described briefly by M. Weber in his paper 'Der Sinn der "Wertfreiheit" der soziologischen und ökonomischen Wissenschaften' (1917), in *Gesammelte Aufsätze zur Wissenschaftslehre*, pp. 496–7. He presents them as means of discussing practical evaluations. Particularly remarkable is his tendency to separate the analytic from the empirical problems.

matter of a much more theoretical and abstract decision, remote from our concrete experiences—but such a choice lays the foundations of order and coherence in our evaluations. Only a constant and watchful confrontation of these two poles may give ground for a hope that the selected value-system will be both consistent and not coldly arbitrary.

The method outlined is similar to the elenctic method of Socrates. He would choose as his point of departure a certain judgement, usually particular, about which his interlocutors were in agreement, and proceed to analyse its presuppositions and implications, exposing in the process the contradictions in the beliefs of his discutants. The disclosure of these contradictions compels us 'to re-examine the correctness of the judgements we laid down as true, and sometimes to revise them or abandon them. The aim of all this process is to bring separate phenomena in the realm of moral standards under one supreme general standard.'[1]

16.4 The fourth method consists in investigating practical consequences of the acceptance of given value-systems. These consequences have, of course, to be studied or predicted by experts. The philosopher would draw conclusions from the result of their work. This is, therefore, a combination of methods two and three. The inquiry may show, for instance, that to realize certain values is in the given circumstances impossible. This might lead to a rejection of the given value-principle.[2] Investigations of the described kind can also lead to a better understanding of the cases when there is a conflict between evaluation and choice; for instance, when one considers best the state of affairs B, but, because of, e.g., its practical unattainability, chooses to aim at a state K.

All this is fairly obvious and procedures of this sort have been applied many times. But one aspect of the problem is notoriously

---

[1] W. Jaeger, *Paideia*, vol. ii (New York, 1943), p. 63.

[2] See K. Mannheim, *Ideology and Utopia*, p. 95: 'Accordingly, from our point of view, an ethical attitude is invalid if it is oriented with reference to norms, with which action in a given historical setting, even with best of intentions, cannot comply. It is invalid then when the unethical action of the individual can no longer be conceived as due to his own personal transgressions, but must be attributed rather to the compulsion of an erroneously founded set of moral axioms.'

ignored. Namely, some value-systems are 'consequentialist', and some are not.[1] When justifying an evaluation within systems of the former type, one invokes the expected outcome of the given act or experience. The content of value-principles in these systems applies to the practical effects: to usefulness, welfare, pleasure. The non-consequentialist systems are based on rules the observance of which is binding and valued irrespectively of the consequences. In those systems value-principles concern ideals such as truth, fidelity, piety, or justice. The standard instances of these two types are utilitarianism and the ethics of honour.

Systems of both types may be generally assessed from the point of view of the consequences of their practical implementation. But care must be taken that truly comprehensive and long-term results are considered. Otherwise, any assessment will be prejudiced, since formulated in the categories of the former, consequentialist and pragmatical type. But this precisely is nowadays the common practice in the Western civilization: we are inclined to look at any value-principles *sub specie* of their more or less immediate consequences (the difference between 'rule' and 'act' utilitarianism is, in this respect, unimportant); and in this way we grant a privileged position to the pragmatic systems, at the expense of the 'strict rules' systems.

In exact sciences, an individual measurement has little to do with establishing the probability of a hypothesis; similarly, while investigating the practical results of the functioning of a value-system we have to take into account not individual cases, and not only even large groups of such cases, but the whole system as historically functioning in a concrete socio-cultural context. Individual acts of honesty may be sometimes painful, difficult, and practically futile; the consequences of universal truth-telling could be embarassing and tormenting to all concerned; but the principles of veracity and honesty have to be surveyed in the wholeness of their working and effects.

The distinction between particular and general consequences links up with that between close and distant consequences. We

[1] This is a simplified statement. Most of the operational systems consist, in fact, of a mixture of both consequentialist and absolute rules. Another important topic for axiological inquiry.

constantly have to remember that man is *the* historical animal, and that little changes and less happens in his life, individual and social, which would not be deeply rooted in his past. Considering only the direct results, even if they are ostensibly unequivocal, we behave like those mothers who are ready to nurse and rock their babies whenever they cry. Of course, the baby usually calms down, the direct result is excellent—but the long-term effect disastrous, since the child learns that crying is rewarded. At a closer look, utilitarianism appears to be a system based on the directly foreseeable consequences, on the principle of maximization of goods whose production has already been mastered: of known benefits, known pleasures. But what about the more distant outcome? The ethics of honour has been criticized, and justly, on the grounds that it very often leads directly to a catastrophe. But seeing it in a historical perspective we have also to consider the fact that it has assisted, in its long and distressful history, in the formation and consolidation of the idea of human dignity. There is in the consequentialist approach a hidden and tacit assumption that desirable effects are produced only by commendable practices—a benign assumption, which reverses the brutal formula of ends justifying means. But it is a sad historical fact that generally approved situations and ideals have often been generated by tortuous and sinister processes.

More challenging and perhaps even more fruitful would be the application of the same method of consequence-testing in the reverse order. Taking as the point of departure a certain state of affairs either accepted as granted or considered desirable, one may investigate which values, if adopted, are likely to favour such a state of affairs; for example, which political values are likely in their observance to further the atmosphere of friendly coexistence between peoples speaking different languages, as we find in Switzerland?

This may seem to be an investigation closed within a vicious circle: we consider the state of affairs D valuable and search for a value likely to generate D. But the described procedure reflects the fact that a principle becomes a value-principle on the basis of choice. And one can support one's choice by reasoning as follows: if I wish to attain D, I have to accept the value-principle delta. Some sociologists and cultural anthropologists indeed maintain that the value of rules of behaviour and evaluation 'consists entirely in their adjustment to the life conditions and the interests of the time and place'.[1] Of course, all these analyses and empirical inquiries have to be historically and socially relativized, because the same principles applied at another time and place bring about different results, and, vice versa, similar states of affairs and objects emerge as result of the implementation of various values. This is most clearly visible in the field of aesthetics.

16.5 The fifth method is similar to the preceding one. It was outlined by Herbert Feigl in his essay *De Principiis Non Disputandum ...?* as the method of 'vindication' in ethics. Feigl writes that 'It consists in showing that adoption of the norms of a given moral system fulfils a purpose.'[2] Developing his idea in the terminology used here, we may say that the method of vindication consists in analysing predictions and promises, implied by value-principles and suggested by the cognitive content, both direct and indirect, of value-judgements.

On the motivational level, values attract us by the visions of the ideal situations they evoke, i.e., by a suggestion that the acceptance of a given value will produce definite, and alluring, situations or states of consciousness. Thus, hedonism is to result in happiness; stoicism—to create a feeling of harmony with the general order of things; realism in art—produce aesthetic satisfaction and a fuller understanding of the life around us. The fifth method, analogous to the method of establishing the 'pragmatic truth' of propositions, purports to check if the given value fulfils its promise and really induces the foretold states of affairs.

A similar method was proposed by May and Abraham Edel, who postulated an appraisal of given value-systems from the point of view of 'human purposes' and 'the matrix of life';[3] this sounds tempting but at the same time abstractly vague.

[1] W. Graham Sumner, *Folkways* (Boston, Mass., 1907), p. 79. Durkheim held a similar opinion. See also M. J. Herskovits, *Man and His Works*, New York, 1948, pp. 76–8.
[2] In *Philosophical Analysis*, ed. M. Black, p. 145.
[3] M. Edel and A. Edel, *Anthropology and Ethics* (Springfield, Ill., 1959), p. 167: '. . . to recognize that the whole system is being developed and used to further certain human purposes, so that, in a different sense from justification

'Self-testing' of a system is analogous to the role of feedback in cybernetics. The input (i.e., values and norms) is to be confronted with output, with the view of correcting the (value)-system, if the obtained results do not meet the aims of this system.

As pointed out above, aesthetic value-principles are comparatively simple to confront with experience. It is easier to advocate aesthetic than other kinds of value, but it is also easier to 'test' and reject them, since they apply to a realm of facts narrower and more accessible than, e.g., ethical principles. Iris Murdoch says: 'Our aesthetics must stand to be judged by great works of art which we know to be such independently; and it is right that our faith in Kant and in Tolstoy should be shaken when we discover shocking eccentricities in their direct judgement of merit in art.'[1] This sounds convincing—of course, if we assume that there was close and necessary links between the general ideas of Kant's or Tolstoy's aesthetics and the particular judgements issued by these thinkers.

16.6 The sixth method is frequently mentioned by moralists, although it is variously defined. It consists in attempting to determine what are the natural and 'normal' needs, propensities, and capabilities of man, and his 'normal' reactions to basic facts of life. Many thinkers, including Marxists, are inclined to believe that human nature displays certain constant characteristics, and that these traits allow us to talk about universal elements of morality. If it is so, then at least some values could be chosen by general consensus.[2]

But at the present stage of our knowledge of man and his environment it seems practically and philosophically prudent to approach the matter in a cautious manner, nicely illustrated by this example given by Sir Isaiah Berlin. I meet a man who likes pushing

within the system, the bases of the system itself may be evaluated in terms of the way it furthers these purposes. No matter how much is incorporated into the system there will still be the matrix of life in which it operates and so of purposes not included in the system.'

[1] I. Murdoch, 'The Sublime and the Good', *Chicago Review* (Autumn 1959), p. 42.

[2] See J. Ladd, *The Structure of a Moral Code*, pp. 179–80.

pins into other people. Pressed for an explanation, he replies finally that

he cannot understand my strange concern—what possible difference can it make whether his pins perforate living men or tennis balls? At this point I begin to suspect that he is in some way deranged. I do not say (with Hume), 'Here is a man with a very different scale of moral values from my own' . . . I rather incline to the belief that the pin-pusher who is puzzled by my questions is to be classified with homicidal lunatics and should be confined in an asylum and not in ordinary prison.[1]

As we know, the criteria of human morality vary depending on time and place. But to expect that philosophers will help in determining values applicable everywhere and always is surely too much. Finding them for here and now, and for the lifespan of the next few generations, is a heavy enough burden. Therefore it is an important task for philosophers to work out, of course with the help of specialists, from psychologists to ecologists, the criteria of normalcy, applicable in the given type of society. (Lawyers do the same, but with a view to eliminating violent conflicts.) Ethology also, this new science combining zoology and anthropology, seems to offer a promise of a fuller and more adequate definition of the natural needs and possibilities of man. With the assistance of these findings and criteria, we may be able to decide who are the people entitled to serve as paradigms in research concerning what is necessary for man and what can be expected of him. (Establishing the so-called 'ethical competence' and granting ethical 'franchise' is an act quite obviously based on a precedent choice of values.)

16.7 Much work of the kind described above has been done, or attempted, on and off, by many philosophers—although the most common method of axiological research is analogous to the usual procedures of decision theory and consists in measuring the immediately involved costs and results of implementing a given principle.

The classics of philosophy contain an enormous wealth of material which can be analysed and explored from the point of view of methods presented here. Many thinkers, such as Hume,

---

[1] I. Berlin, 'Rationality of Value Judgements', in *Rational Decisions*, ed. Friedrich, pp. 221–3.

Shaftesbury, and Marx, have utilized the results of particular disciplines; Aristotle, Epictetus, Spinoza, Scheler, and Nicolai Hartmann arranged value-systems; Plato, Hobbes, and Nietzsche observed the consequences of accepting particular values; many Christian philosophers, like St. Augustine and Pascal, pondered whether the promises implied by the system accepted by them materialize; the idea of the 'natural man' was for Locke and Rousseau the cornerstone of their axiologies.

§17. *The function of the philosophy of value*

17.1 Philosophers who concentrate on the logical analysis of value-judgements are often accused of moral indifference; of disregarding what are really the fundamental problems of axiology, the problems centred around the simple question of how to live; of ignoring essential issues and dealing only with axiological 'technology'; and at least of a relativism bordering on nihilism.

As I have said above, methodological relativism is a requisite component of the equipment of an axiologist. It is impossible to analyse the content of various value-systems without penetrating their immanent structure and recognizing that they are ruled by their own laws. A philosopher-analyst uses in his scrutiny the same technique as the philologist who, studying various national languages, accepts their internal rules as immanently justified, and does not claim that, e.g., English phonetics rests on a mutilation of the 'normal' speech sounds, or that the definite particle in German signals a confusion concerning the gender of things.

But methodological relativism does not have to be coupled with indifference. Logical analysis of evaluation may—and ought to, if philosophy is to carry on its traditional cultural functions—prepare the ground for answering the questions: which values to choose? To be sure, philosophers have been compelled to say good-bye to the age-long hope that they will discover a certain road to unquestionably true answers. (Clinging to the idea of one demonstrably true and universally applicable set of values may be seen as a result of the fear of freedom: that our responsibility increases in direct ratio to the growth of our freedom is a disturbing thought to very many.) Values cannot be safely deduced from empirical data and the rules of logic: they have to be *chosen*. And they should be chosen with consideration given to possibly everything, to the practically infinite number of facts past, present, and foreseeable.

The philosopher cannot choose for anybody. But his social duty, imposed on him by the great heritage of his over-arching discipline, is to assist in this most difficult and arduous of human tasks. His help can be twofold: (1) he may elaborate conceptual tools and working techniques applicable in evaluative reasoning and in analysis of evaluative processes; (2) he may make men more fully aware of the variety of their possible choices and of the ways these choices can be accomplished and justified.

The first task belongs to analytic philosophy; the other is to some extent fulfilled by the teachings of the classics, and by the 'speculative' philosophers, moralists, advocates of particular value-systems. Both types of philosophizing and influencing men may be really fruitful only if they mutually supplement each other. Analysis without vision is barren; vision without analysis—hazy and dangerous. I am convinced, however, that at the present stage the analytic tasks of the philosophy of value are paramount. Not only because there is hardly ever a dearth of eager prophets and preachers. Also because speculative tendencies have for long dominated ethics and aesthetics, and modern analytic trends in axiology would frequently result either in irrationalism, or in an artificial separation of philosophy from science, or in some blend of these two tendencies.

17.2 The maieutic method of Socrates—the father of European ethics, and of axiology in general—not only constituted one of his means of doing philosophy, but also determined the basic function of a philosopher: to help men in becoming aware of the knowledge they possess. That was supposed to be the role of philosophy at the time when specialized sciences had not yet evolved and the whole of knowledge resided latent in the heads of thinking people. Today, when the wealth of human knowledge has become literally immense and un-commandable, the maieutic method in philosophy again become singularly attractive. The sciences 'possess the true knowledge', the general and comprehensive meaning of which 'men are not aware of' and 'have to be helped to it' by the method of 'a common search'. 'The role of a director consists in an expert asking of questions', and 'pressing for answers'.[1] This characterization of the maieutic method aptly formulates the demands we should put to the contemporary philosophy of values.

17.3 Before we wind up our investigations, we have yet to tackle a problem of primary importance: is the conceptual framework, presented in the first three chapters of this book, axiologically neutral? More precisely: would this conceptual framework influence the behaviour of its users? I think that an absolute axiological neutrality is an unattainable ideal for two reasons.

First, any attempt to systematize a conceptual framework applicable to evaluations, any attempt to methodize evaluation itself, and any effort to make the choice of values more conscious and mentally controlled, furthers a shrinking of the scope of unconscious, incoherent, and inconsiderate evaluations and choices. Introducing a certain order into our thinking about values and evaluation, although it can and ought to be free from an immediate moral intent, is not an axiologically neutral activity. Fuller awareness and coherence are not natural facts, but results of choice—or, in other words, values.

Undertaking such attempts and efforts, a philosopher of value follows the same route as do all scholars in the humanities and in law, who also tacitly adopt the assumption that men wish to observe in their behaviour a reasonable consistency. When we spend time and energy on analysing "x is honest', or 'y is beautiful', we assume not only that such utterances are worth investigating, but also that their mutual relations are somehow relevant. And they are relevant only if we take it that men wish, or at least ought to wish, to follow in their evaluations some predictable patterns. But Predictability, that goddess of science, is also a value.

The conceptual scheme proposed in this book is founded on the assumptions that for evaluative utterances in form of sentences the informative function is more important than the expressive, and that the primary point of evaluative discourse is not to reveal and enforce one's opinions, but to communicate. These assumptions, which I have tried to substantiate, are not, in their effect, axiologically neutral.

[1] W. Tatarkiewicz, *Historia filozofii*, 5th ed. (Warsaw, 1958), vol. i, p. 95.

Secondly, a philosopher co-operating, however wisely, in a choice of values, does not work in a void. The range of values from among which we may choose and which the philosopher analyses, is always determined by the given physical, social, political, and technological possibilities, and also limited to these systems of evaluation which are currently present in human consciousness. Their scope is, therefore, historically changeable and in each case finite. The functioning systems of evaluation constitute powerful motivational wholes, which attract most of man's attention. The actual choices are usually confined to only a few real or imaginary possibilities. Of course, the philosopher's task is to broaden their range, but he cannot transcend his own reach. And the beliefs concerning what is and what is not empirically knowable and testable, concerning the grounds and methods of particular scientific disciplines, concerning human nature—thus the beliefs which form the foundations of the above described (§16.1–§16.6) methods of validating the choice of values—demarcate the philosopher's horizons.

To escape normativeness is, therefore, impossible. It is possible, though, to tame and keep it under some control. It ought not to take the form of undeclared assumptions, but to be restricted to the effects of the functioning of the analysed and construed concepts.

Definitions of limbs sprained or dislocated, of burns of first, second, or third degree, adopted in medicine, have their normative effects, i.e., they influence in a specific way the behaviour of surgeons and patients. In legal procedure, a normative function is performed by the definitions, spelled out in the highway code, of a vehicle, a public road, severe bodily damage. And, of course, these definitions have been formulated with a full consciousness of their future normative use. But their content has been determined not by a normative intention, but by the findings of the given discipline. On the basis of their experience and research, physicians classify kinds of bodily damage into 'light' and 'severe'; their classification forms the basis of definitions. For a policeman, who investigates a car accident, these definitions will function normatively: on their ground he will decide what to do with the culprit.

To take the issue more broadly still, any scientific conceptual system, be it in biology or in physics, covers only a certain limited range of classes of objects and facts. Even if open to admit new members, it is open only to a certain degree, and otherwise closed. This closedness has not, however, to be based on an initial *exclusion* of certain phenomena, but results from the very structure of human conceptual thinking. The normative impact of these conceptual systems, visible, e.g., in the choice of topics for research and in experimental methods, is not an impact anticipated from the start and in principle.

Concepts, arguments, and reasonings, analysed by philosophers, also inescapably influence the people who make use of these analyses. But normativeness flows in both directions: a change in the functioning of concepts influences their philosophical analysis, even the method of analysis. Unrealized or half-realized normativeness of value philosophy is mainly a result of that pressure of the object of analysis: language and behaviour. Sometimes philosophers seem to be hypnotized, like birds by snakes, by their object of scrutiny.

To sum up, in one plain sentence, what has been said above about the choice of values and normativeness: a philosopher is only a man and in performing his human tasks he is restricted to his human resources.

§18. *Conclusion*

18.1 The contemporary axiologist is in the situation of a man who has accidentally strayed into the stands of a sports ground and watches the behaviour of men, running on the field after a ball. Their movements are chaotic; the game is fast and bewilderingly complicated; no one of the spectators can answer the question what the rules of the game are and whether there are indeed any rules to it. It seems that some players observe the principles of soccer, others of rugby, still others of handball; the antics of the rest are describable in terms of none of these games. Repeatedly, an emerging semblance of order is drowned in what looks like a general mess. Occasionally the game becomes quite rough and the stretcher-bearers have a lot of work to do; but more and more players arrive and the spectacle goes on.

Many twentieth-century philosophers have reached the conclusion that what they are watching is not a game at all, but a massive, spontaneous letting-off of steam. The role of an axiologist, they say, is to describe the behaviour of particular players, or to compute statistics concerning a greater number of them; and not to analyse, explain, or codify their behaviour which is not a game in the sense of being subject to some definite set of rules.

I do not think such an attitude of resigned neutralism is correct. It is excessively rigid and based on a dogmatic differentiation of the rational and irrational, and of description and evaluation. More importantly, it tacitly presupposes that the players of the game of life not only do not observe any rules, but do not wish to know and apply them. In other words, it is assumed that when men utter evaluations, they express their emotions and moods, or want to impress others and induce them to do something—but that they neither use nor wish to use any general rules of evaluation; that in evaluating they neither do nor wish to pass factual information.

The growing number of coexisting, competing, and warring value-systems, and above all the difficulties in and disagreements about the appropriate conceptual apparatus to analyse evaluative utterances, resulted in a peculiar demonization of evaluational phenomena. Many philosophers and scientists have decided to shrug them off as erratic and inscrutable. Several attempts to counteract this development resulted in more or less traditional forms of axiological dogmatism. But another tendency seems to be more characteristic: the tendency to reflect, in the very method of philosophizing, the accidentality and shapelessness of evaluations in modern mass society. It is most clearly visible in 'linguistically' oriented philosophy, which aims at studying 'speech acts', at following as closely as possible the convolutions of common language, at describing in painstakingly subtle ways the peculiarities of verbal usage. Many merits of this approach are indisputable, but we ought to remember that human culture has originated in and evolved through the imperious activity of imposing order on the messy tangle of facts and things. Putting on one level the quirks of common speech and the rules of logic involves a renunciation of an essential part of man's intellectual tradition.

18.2 The conceptual and methodological proposals, expressed in this book, are designed to point a way out of the impasse of axiological agnosticism without blundering again into some kind of axiological fideism. Let me briefly summarize the main elements of the proposed conceptual scheme.

'*Evaluation*' may signify either a kind of psychological process—an evaluative experience, expressed or unexpressed—or a kind of reasoning, a discursive evaluation. Evaluation-experiences form the *motivational* pattern of evaluation; evaluation-reasonings, the *theoretical* pattern.

What is the difference between evaluation and *description*? Descriptive statements are ultimately substantiated by reference to the accepted laws and findings of science; value-judgements are substantiated by reference to general evaluative assumptions. The line between both types of statements is moveable, and is determined by both the beliefs about the scientific or unscientific character of given opinions or theories (concerning, e.g., human nature, or harmony), and the scope of the given value-system (which may, or may not, include, for instance, rules concerning man's behaviour towards animals).

The term *value* is used in at least three different senses, which were named *attributive*, *quantitative*, and *axiological*. Value in the attributive sense is a thing or property, to which valuableness is ascribed; in the quantitative sense, a measurable quantity of what determines value (two pence as the value of an egg); in the axiological sense, an idea which ascribes value to certain objects, properties, or events. The definition of the axiological value within the theoretical pattern of evaluation is: M is an axiological value if and only if M is a judgement, ascribing the quality of valuableness to objects, properties, or states of affairs, and constituting within the given value-system a final justification of other judgements of the system. Within the motivational pattern: whatever is the strongest or ultimate motivational factor in X's behaviour, overt or mental, is for X a value. The proposition, concerning an axiological value, is expressed in a statement, named a *value-principle*.

A value-principle, or, more often, a set of interconnected value-principles, the empirical criteria bound with them—which make it possible to distinguish valuable from valueless objects—and the value-judgements, based on principles and criteria, form a *value-system*. Such a system is expressed in a corresponding *value-language*, within which specific rules of signification and inference obtain. Within a national language there may coexist many separate or related value-languages.

Value-judgements should be interpreted within the terms of the value-languages to which they belong. Only then may they be fully comprehended and only then do they have a logical value, i.e., are either true or false.

The range of the cognitive content, communicated by a value-judgement, depends on whether and to what extent we know the given value-language. This content is of two kinds: *directly* expressed and *indirectly* transmitted or suggested. The direct cognitive content of a value-judgement concerns primarily the position which the given object occupies on the scale determined by values and criteria of the given value-system. Thus it informs about the relative place of the evaluated object among other objects, to which the same values and criteria may apply, and in doing that it 'arranges' the whole class of such objects. Besides, the more specific the predicate of the judgement, the more information the judgement contains about the empirical characteristics of the evaluated object. The indirect cognitive content of a judgement may be stated in the form of a hypothetical prognosis, which concerns the probable reaction to the evaluated object or fact on the part of men belonging to the same cultural milieu. Thus the direct cognitive content may be said to apprehend the object synchronically, and the indirect diachronically.

To evaluate is both to inform and to influence. The effects of value-judgements are observed on the level of the motivational pattern of evaluation. The cognitive content of value-judgements is the basis of their motivational appeal; but while motivational impact unsupported by the comprehending of a judgement would be purely adventitious, it is quite possible to understand a judgement theoretically without being influenced by it—in this manner we understand judgements contained in historical or anthropological documents.

In human life, value-judgements play the role of order-introducing factors. However, since in comparison to the wealth of 'arrangeable' objects and facts the number of arranging instruments, i.e., evaluative predicates, is rather limited, and since the criteria of assessment are only infrequently explained, to understand a given value-judgement adequately it is essential to know its situational context. With ethical value-judgements, we become aware of that context placing the assessed act within the given time and milieu; with aesthetic judgements the context is formed by anticipations held with regard to the appraised object.

18.3 The proposed set of concepts has to serve two aims. First, to facilitate communication between specialists, investigating the problems of evaluation within their respective disciplines, and thus, in other words, to facilitate an integration of the sciences of man. Second, to assist in generating methods of a discursive validation of the choice of values.

The philosophers of value of a logico-empirical persuasion are sometimes accused of fostering nihilism, which is alleged to follow inescapably from methodological relativism and a rejection of the existence of objective and universal values. Another accusation is that they conduct their analyses *ad usum delphini*. The last chapter of this book aims at warding off such charges. It outlines the role of the philosopher of value as a Socratic midwife, who co-operates with scientific–specialists in investigating the numerous aspects of valuation and choice. Six methods which a philosopher may use in helping to validate a choice of values are described. These methods are based on the assumption that there exists a broad understanding and exchange of information between the social, psychological, and medical sciences, and the humanities. Therefore the attaining of the first end depends on the success in achieving the second. Thus the purported function of this book is technical and assisting, similar to the role of a linguist and grammarian, who systematizes the vocabulary and structure of a given national language not to make it more detached from other languages, but to facilitate international communication of ideas.

18.4 In continuation of this linguistic simile, let us recall the standard division of semiotics into semantics, syntactics, and pragmatics. Like signs, statements may also be seen as studied in these three aspects: the equivalent of semantics will be investigating the relation between the statement and its object; of syntactics, analysing the relation between a given statement and other statements; of pragmatics, studying the relation between a statement and its users. For the last fifty years evaluation has been studied mainly in its pragmatical aspect, and more precisely in the aspect of the relation between the evaluator and the evaluative utterance. The distinction between description and evaluation has been analysed also primarily from that point of view. In this book the expressive function of evaluation, thoroughly investigated and overvalued, has been given little attention.

The differentiation between description and evaluation is here attempted by means of 'syntactics', i.e., of finding out what is the relation to other statements of, respectively, descriptive statements and value-judgements. I have been dealing with 'pragmatics' only as much as it concerns the motivational impact of value-judgements. Most space and attention is given to 'semantics'— i.e., to investigating the relation between a judgement and its object.

Thus, value-judgements are treated in this book as statements in which we communicate not only our emotions, but primarily our thoughts about the relations between men and their environment.

BIBLIOGRAPHY

AJDUKIEWICZ, K., *Język i poznanie*, 2 vols. Warsaw, 1960.

ALBERT, ETHEL M., 'The Classification of Values', *American Anthropologist*, vol. lviii (1965).

ARROW, KENNETH J., *Social Choice and Individual Values*, 2nd ed. New York, 1963.

ASCHENBRENNER, K., *The Concepts of Value: Foundation of Value Theory*. Dordrecht, 1971.

AUSTIN, J. L., *How to Do Things with Words*. Oxford, 1962.

AYER, SIR ALFRED J., *Language, Truth, and Logic*. London, 1946.

— *Philosophical Essays*. London, 1959.

BAIER, KURT, *The Moral Point of View*. Ithaca, N.Y., 1958.

BAYLIS, C. A., 'Grading ,Values, and Choice', *Mind*, 1958.

BEARDSLEY, MONROE C., *Aesthetics*, New York, 1958.

BENEDICT, RUTH, *Patterns of Culture*. London, 1935.

BERENSON, BERNARD, *The Florentine Painters of the Renaissance*. Boston, Mass., 1896.

BERLIN, SIR ISAIAH, 'Equality', *Proceedings of the Aristotelian Society* (1955–6).

BLACK, MAX, *The Labyrinth of Language*. Harmondsworth, Middx., 1968.

— *Language and Philosophy*. Ithaca, N.Y., 1944.

— ed., *Philosophical Analysis*. Ithaca, N.Y., 1959.

BURKE, EDMUND, 'A Philosophical Inquiry into the Origin of our Ideas of the Sublime and the Beautiful', *Works*, vol. i. London, 1902.

BURTT, EDWIN A., *The Metaphysical Foundations of Modern Physical Science*. Chicago, 1924.

BUTTERFIELD, H., *The Origins of Modern Physical Science*. London, 1950.

CARNAP, R., *The Logical Syntax of Language*. London, 1937.

— *Philosophy and Logical Syntax*. London, 1935.

CLARK, SIR KENNETH, *The Gothic Revival*, 2nd edn. London, 1950.

CLASSEN, P., '"Charientic" Judgements', *Philosophy* (April 1958).

COFER, C. N., and M. H. APPLEY, *Motivation: Theory and Research*. New York, 1964.

CROCE, B., *Aesthetic*, transl. D. Ainslie. London, 1922.

CZEŻOWSKI, TADEUSZ, *Filozofia na rozdrożu*. Warsaw, 1965.

DE GEORGE, R. T., ed., *Ethics and Society*. Garden City, N.J., 1966.

DEWEY, J., *The Quest for Certainty*. New York, 1929.

DROBNITSKI, O. G., *Mir ozshivshikh predmetov. Problema tsennosti i marksistskaya filosofia*. Moscow, 1967.

DUBISLAV, W., 'Zur Unbegründbarkeit der Forderungssätze'. *Theoria*, iii. (1937).

DUPRÉEL, E., *Traité de morale*. Brussels, 1932.

DURKHEIM, E., *Sociology and Philosophy*, transl. D. F. Pocock. London, 1953.

EDEL, M. and A., *Anthropology and Ethics*. Springfield, Ill., 1959.

EDWARDS, PAUL, *The Logic of Moral Discourse*. New York, 1955.

EHRENFELS, C. VON, *System der Werttheorie*, 2 vols. Leipzig, 1897–8.

ELTON, W., ed., *Aesthetics and Language*. Oxford, 1954.

ELZENBERG, H., *Wartość i człowiek*. Toruń, 1966.

FOOT, PHILIPPA, *Theories of Ethics*. Oxford, 1967.

FRANK, P., *Philosophy of Science*. Garden City, N.J., 1957.

FRIEDRICH, C. J., *Rational Decisions*. New York, 1964.

FRITZHAND, M., *W kręgu etyki marksistowskiej*. Warsaw, 1966.

FRONDIZI, RISIERI, *What is Value?* La Salle, Ill., 1963.

GEYMONAT, LUDOVICO, *Filosofia e filosofia della scienza*. Milan, 1960.

GLASS, B., *Science and Ethical Values*. Chapel Hill, N.C., 1965.

GOLDMANN, LUCIEN, *The Human Sciences and Philosophy*. London, 1969.

GOMBRICH, E. H., *Art and Illusion*, London, 1960.

— *Meditations on a Hobby Horse*. London, 1963.

GOODMAN, N., *Languages of Art*. Indianapolis, 1968.

GROSSE, E., *Die Anfänge der Kunst*. Freiburg and Leipzig, 1894.

HALLDÉN, SÖREN, *Emotive Propositions*. Stockholm, 1954.

HANDY, ROLLO, *Value Theory and the Behavioral Sciences*, Springfield, Ill., 1969.

HARE, R. M., *Freedom and Reason*. Oxford, 1963.

— *The Language of Morals*, Oxford, 1952.

HARTMAN, R. S., 'A Logical Definition of Value', *Journal of Philosophy* (1952).

HARTMANN, N., *Ethics*, transl. Stanton Coit, vol. i. London, 1932.

HAUSER, A., *The Social History of Art*. New York, 1957.

HILLIARD, A. L., *The Forms of Value*. New York, 1950.

HINTIKKA, J., *Knowledge and Belief*. Ithaca, N.Y., 1962.

HOMANS, G., *Social Behavior*. New York, 1961.

HOSPERS, J., *Human Conduct : An Introduction to the Problems of Ethics*. New York, 1961.

HOWE, I., *William Faulkner*. New York, 1951.

HUIZINGA, JOHAN, *The Waning of the Middle Ages*, trans. F. Hopman. London, 1924.

HUDSON, W. D., ed., *The Is/Ought Question*. London, 1969.

HUME, DAVID, *A Treatise of Human Nature*. Everyman's Library, London, 1911.

INGARDEN, ROMAN, *Przeżycie, dzieło, wartość*. Cracow, 1966. Also in German: *Erlebnis, Kunstwerk und Wert*. Tübingen, 1969.

— *Studia z estetyki*, 2 vols. Warsaw, 1958.

JAEGER, W., *Paideia*, 3 vols. New York, 1943.

JAMES, WILLIAM, *The Varieties of Religious Experience*. London, 1902.

KEESING, F. M., *Cultural Anthropology*. New York, 1958.

KLUCKHOHN, CLYDE, 'Values and Value-Orientations in the Theory of Action: An Exploration in Definition and Classification', in T. Parsons and E. A. Shils, eds., *Toward a General Theory of Action*. Cambridge, Mass., 1951.

KLIBANSKY, R., ed., *Philosophy at the Mid-Century*, vol. iii. Florence, 1958.

KMITA, JERZY, 'Problem wartości logicznej ocen', *Studia Filozoficzne* (1964), No. 1.

— 'Wartości i oceny', *Studia Filozoficzne* (1968), No. 1.

KONORSKI, JERZY, *Integrative Activity of the Brain*. Chicago, 1967.

KRAUS, OSCAR, *Die Werttheorien. Geschichte und Kritik*. Brünn, 1937.

KROEBER, A., ed., *Anthropology Today*. Chicago, 1953.

LADD, JOHN, *The Structure of a Moral Code*. Cambridge, Mass., 1957.

LAFLEUR, L. J., 'Biological Evidence in Aesthetics', *Philosophical Review*, xi. (1942).

LAMONT, W. D., *The Value Judgement*. Edinburgh, 1955.

LAVELLE, L., *Traité des valeurs*, 2 vols. Paris, 1915.

LEPLEY, RAY, ed., *The Language of Value*. New York, 1957.

— ed., *Value: A Cooperative Inquiry*. New York, 1949.

LEVI, A. W., 'The Trouble with Ethics: Values, Method, and the Search for Moral Norms', *Mind* (April 1961).

LEVICH, M., *Aesthetics and the Philosophy of Criticism*. New York, 1963.

LÉVI-STRAUSS, CLAUDE, *La Pensée sauvage*. Paris, 1962.

— 'The Structural Study of Myth', *Journal of American Folklore* (1955), No. 270.

LEWIS, C. I., *An Analysis of Knowledge and Evaluation*. La Salle, Ill., 1947.

LHOTE, H., *Peintures préhistoriques des Sahara*. Paris, 1958.

LIDDELL, H. G., and R. S. SCOTT, *A Greek-English Lexicon*. Oxford, 1925.

LORENZ, K., *On Aggression*. London, 1967.

LUNDBERG, G., 'Semantics and the Value Problem'. *Social Forces* (1948).

LUTYŃSKI, J., 'O wartościowaniu i manichejskiej, postawie w naukach społecznych', *Kultura i Społeczeństwo* (1958), No. 4.

MACINTYRE, A., *A Short History of Ethics*. New York, 1966.

MALEWSKI, A., *O zastosowaniach teorii zachowania*. Warsaw, 1964.

MANNHEIM, KARL, *Essays in Sociology and Social Psychology*. London, 1953.

— *Ideology and Utopia*. London, 1936.

MARTIN, R. M., *Toward a Systematic Pragmatic*. Amsterdam, 1959.

MEINECKE, FRIEDRICH, 'Kausalitäten und Werte in der Geschichte' (first publ. 1928), in *Staat und Persönlichkeit*. Berlin, 1933.

MEYER, L. B., 'Some Remarks on Value and Greatness in Music', *Journal of Aesthetics and Art Criticism* (June 1959).

MOORE, G. E., *Principia Ethica*, Cambridge, 1903.

MURDOCH, IRIS, 'The Sublime and the Good', *Chicago Review* (Autumn 1959).

MYRDAL, GUNNAR, *The Political Element in the Development of Economic Theory*. London, 1953.

NOWAK, L., *U podstaw marksistowskiej aksjologii*. Warsaw, 1974.

NOWELL SMITH, P. H., *Ethics*. Harmondsworth, Middx., 1954.

NUTTIN, J., *La Structure de la personnalité*. Paris, 1965.

OGDEN, C. K., and I. A. RICHARDS, *The Meaning of Meaning*. New York, 1938.

OSBORNE, HAROLD, *Theory of Beauty*. London, 1952.

OSSOWSKA, M., *Podstawy nauki o moralności*. Warsaw, 1947.

— 'Rola ocen w kształtowaniu pojęć', in *Fragmenty filozoficzne, księga pamiątkowa ku czci T. Kotarbińskiego*. Warsaw, 1967.

— *Socjologia moralności*. Warsaw, 1963.

OSSOWSKI, S. *U podstaw estetyki*, 1st ed., 1932; 3rd ed. Warsaw, 1958.

— 'Z dociekań nad genezą sztuki', *Wiedza i Życie* (1938).

PALMER, R. B., and R. HAMERTON-KELLY, eds., *Philomathes. Studies and Essays in the Humanities in Memory of Philip Merlan*. The Hague, 1971.

PARSONS, T., and E. A. SHILS, eds., *Toward a General Theory of Action*. Cambridge, Mass., 1951.

PATER, WALTER, *Appreciations*. London, 1907.

— *The Renaissance*. London, 1904.

PEPPER, S. C., *The Work of Art*. Bloomington, Ind., 1955.

PERRY, R. B., *General Theory of Value*. Cambridge, Mass., 1926.

— *Realms of Value*. Cambridge, Mass., 1954.

PETERS, R. S., *The Concept of Motivation*. London, 1958.

PETRAŻYCKI, L., *Wstęp do nauki prawa i moralności*. Warsaw, 1930.

PIAGET, J., *The Moral Judgment of the Child*, transl. M. Gabain. New York, 1962.

PLATT, J. R., 'How we see Straight Lines', *Scientific American* (January 1962).

POINCARÉ, H., *Dernières pensées*. Paris, 1913.

POPPER, SIR KARL, *Conjectures and Refutations*. London, 1963.

PRZEŁĘCKI, M., 'Filozoficzne konsekwencje semantycznej teorii prawdy', *Studia Filozoficzne* (1973), No. 6.

READ, H., *Education through Art*. London, 1934.

RESCHER, NICHOLAS, *Introduction to Value Theory*. Englewood Cliffs, N.J., 1969.

— *The Logic of Commands*. London, 1966.

— *Topics in Philosophical Logic*. Dordrecht, 1968.

RICHARDS, I. A., *Principles of Literary Criticism*. London, 1924.

ROSS, A., 'Imperatives and Logic', *Philosophy of Science* (1944).

RYLE, GILBERT, *The Concept of Mind*. London, 1949.

SIBLEY, F., 'Aesthetics and the Look of Things', *Journal of Philosophy* (1959).

SKEAT, W. W., *An Etymological Dictionary of the English Language*. Oxford, 1879.

SCHELER, M., *Der Formalismus in der Ethik und die materiale Wertethik*. 2nd ed. Halle, 1921.

SCHILPP, P. A., ed., *The Philosophy of Rudolf Carnap*. New York, 1963.

SCHLICK, MORITZ, *Problems of Ethics*. New York, 1962.

SESONSKE, A., 'On the Skepticism of "Ethics and Language"', *Journal of Philosophy*, No. 20 (1953).

SŁAWSKI, F., *Słownik etymologiczny języka polskiego*. Cracow, 1965.

SPINOZA, B., *Ethic*, transl. W. Hale White. Oxford, 1927.

STEBBING, L. SUSAN, *Thinking to Some Purpose*. Harmondsworth, Middx., 1945.

STEVENSON, CHARLES L., *Ethics and Language*. New Haven, Conn., 1944.

— *Facts and Values*. New Haven, Conn., 1963.

SUMNER, W. GRAHAM, *Folkways*. Boston, Mass., 1907.

TAINE, H., *La Philosophie de l'art*. Paris, 1865.

TATARKIEWICZ, W., *Droga do filozofii*. Warsaw, 1971.

— *Historia filozofii*, 5th edn., 3 vols. Warsaw, 1958.

TISELIUS, A., and S. NILSSON, eds., *The Place of Value in a World of Facts*, Nobel Symposium 14 (1969). Stockholm, 1970.

TOPOLSKI, J., *Metodologia historii*. Warsaw, 1968.

TOULMIN, STEPHEN, *The Place of Reason in Ethics*. London, 1948.

TRILLING, LIONEL, *The Opposing Self*. London, 1955.

URMSON, J. O., *The Emotive Theory of Ethics*. London, 1968.
— 'On Grading', *Mind* (1950).
VON WRIGHT, G. H., *The Varieties of Goodness*. London, 1963.
WALLIS, MIECZYSŁAW, *Przeżycie i wartość*. Cracow, 1968.
WARNOCK, M., *Ethics since 1900*. London, 1960.
WEBER, MAX, *Gesammelte Aufsätze zur Religionssoziologie*. Tübingen, 1920.
— *Gesammelte Aufsätze zur Wissenschaftslehre*. Tübingen, 1951.
WELDON, T. D., *The Vocabulary of Politics*. Harmondsworth, Middx., 1953.
WILSON, E., *Classics and Commercials*. New York, 1962.
WIND, EDGAR. *Art and Anarchy*. London, 1963.
WITTGENSTEIN, L., *Philosophical Investigations*. Oxford, 1953.
WOJNAR, I., *Esthétique et pédagogique*. Paris, 1962.
ZINK, S., *The Concepts of Ethics*. London, 1962.

INDEX